Praise for *Refilling*

A wise and playful guide to living w
others. Forging insight from her own experiences as pastor, mother, spouse, and human, Brenda Bos invites us to experience caregiving as a spiritual journey that can shape us into healthier, less exhausted, more vibrant versions of ourselves. Written with humor, candor, and humility, *Refilling the Reservoirs* offers much-needed support and strategies for sustaining ourselves. Reading it is like relaxing over coffee with a smart, caring, honest friend who always has our best interests in mind.

—**Duane R. Bidwell**, author of *After the Worst Day Ever: What Sick Kids Know about Sustaining Hope in Chronic Illness*

With a measure of humor and a full dose of honesty, Brenda Bos invites weary caregivers into brave spaces for some serious reflection. Readers will appreciate the conversational tone and relatable stories. Bos's earnest care for those readers is felt from the first page to the last.

—**Shauna Hannan**, professor of preaching, Pacific Lutheran Theological Seminary; author of *The Peoples' Sermon: Preaching as a Ministry of the Whole Congregation* and coauthor of *Scripting a Sermon: Using the Wisdom of Filmmaking for Impactful Preaching*

How do we lean into faith, into God, to help us navigate and embrace the chaos, see the beauty in the struggle, and open our hearts toward healing? In this transformative experience, Brenda Bos takes her readers on a journey of deep inner reflection toward hope, restoration, and freedom. Bos's willingness to be vulnerable—to share her heart, mind, and life experiences—is transformative. Thank you, Brenda Bos, for showing your readers that we are not alone and there is hope.

—**Jill Mattinson-Cruz**, adoption program supervisor

Refilling

THE

Reservoirs

Refilling

THE

Reservoirs

Spiritual Care

for the

Exhausted

Caregiver

Brenda Bos

FORTRESS PRESS
MINNEAPOLIS

REFILLING THE RESERVOIRS
Spiritual Care for the Exhausted Caregiver

Copyright © 2025 Fortress Press. All rights reserved. Except for brief
quotations in critical articles and reviews, no part of this book may be
reproduced in any manner without prior written permission from the
publisher. Email copyright@fortresspress.com or write to Permissions,
Fortress Press, PO Box 1209, Minneapolis, MN 55440-1209.

All Scripture quotations, unless otherwise indicated, are from the New
Revised Standard Version Bible, copyright © 1989 National Council of the
Churches of Christ in the United States of America. Used by permission. All
rights reserved worldwide.

29   28   27   26   25   24   1   2   3   4   5   6   7   8   9

Library of Congress Cataloging-in-Publication Data

Names: Bos, Brenda, author.
Title: Refilling the reservoirs : spiritual care for the exhausted
  caregiver / Brenda Bos.
Description: Minneapolis : Fortress Press, [2025]
Identifiers: LCCN 2024025690 (print) | LCCN 2024025691 (ebook) | ISBN
  9798889832188 (print) | ISBN 9798889832195 (ebook)
Subjects: LCSH: Spiritual care (Medical care) | Caregivers--Religious
  aspects.
Classification: LCC BL65.M4 B677 2025 (print) | LCC BL65.M4 (ebook) | DDC
  259--dc23/eng/20240805
LC record available at https://lccn.loc.gov/2024025690
LC ebook record available at https://lccn.loc.gov/2024025691

Cover design: Brad Norr
Cover image: Flowing water with air bubbles, from Yuri Samsonov/
Shutterstock

Print ISBN: 979-8-8898-3218-8
eBook ISBN: 979-8-8898-3219-5

For the Saturday morning support group

Contents

Introduction—Refilling the Reservoirs   1

1. Chaos   9

2. Loss of Home   21

3. Guilt   31

4. Loss of Self-Identity   37

5. Isolation   45

6. Anger   51

7. Knowledge   57

8. Time   63

9. Wrestling   71

10. Meaning   83

11. Pause   89

12. Gratitude   95

13. Hope   103

14. Forgiveness   111

15. Complete Surrender   119

16. The Search for God   127

Acknowledgments   133

Introduction—Refilling the Reservoirs

Two o'clock in the morning: young parents sleep fitfully while their newborn stirs in the next room. We hear gentle crying, which gets louder. It is not the infant; it is one of the parents. Overwhelmed, frightened, exhausted. Now the baby begins to cry, hungry, cold, wet, pick any of the maladies that wake a babe in the dark of night. The second parent now wakes, hears the baby, nudges their partner, "You go," but the first parent, so exhausted, sobs and says they just do not have it in them. The second sits up, half-asleep, realizing the two people they love most in the world are now wailing. Before they know it, all three are crying.

In another part of the town, Sheila unlocks the car for Rocky, her husband of forty-seven years, and helps him get into the car. Rocky wears pajama pants and slippers. He was not meant to go shopping at this hour. Sheila needed an antacid in the middle of the night, but since Rocky's diagnosis, she cannot leave him alone, not even for a moment. Rocky pulls two candy bars and a can of shaving cream out of his hoodie pocket. They have not paid for any of these items; he has helped himself to them, innocently, as he usually does. Sheila has had to go back into stores for months, meekly explaining her husband has Alzheimer's disease and likely intended to pay for any pinched items, but it slipped his mind. She is about to go back into the store, but it is almost 3 a.m., and she is exhausted. She has to weigh her options: return the stolen items or drive away and risk arrest. "Maybe jail would be better than this," she thinks, and immediately hates herself.

Two hours later an alarm clock rings. Pat hits the alarm, cursing the 4:30 a.m. start. But this is the time needed to get up and get ready before getting up the kids. Pat's head hurts, as it does most mornings. By 6 a.m. the kids are up, moving too slowly, but they get into the car by seven and to school. Pat is at work by 7:30 a.m., needing to work four hours before picking up Dad for a doctor's appointment. Pat yells at the doctor, yells in traffic, yells at the kids. Pat cannot remember a day when there was no yelling.

All over the city, all over the planet, people are at the end of their ropes. Good-hearted, well-meaning people who meant it when they said, " 'Till death do us part" are realizing they do not have the strength to go on. Parents are out of ideas, young people are tapped out, seniors spend their days enraged or resentful. This reduced state did not come from our environmental crisis, the fear of war or Covid-19, although these issues have not helped. Instead, many people are struggling under the burden of caring, the weight of loving. Humans who willingly, joyfully agreed to be in relationship with other humans now realize they do not have the ability to continue the care. This is a frightening, embarrassing admission to make. But we are out of gas. The reservoir of love and patience is long-ago drained.

Some people will turn to therapists or trainers or friends to talk about this depletion. Others will not, because, let's be honest, nothing is going to change, so why ask for help? And so, the cycle of despair continues. Despair may be too strong of a word to describe these feelings. Despair requires energy to be felt. Many of us are just numb, not able to name any emotions.

Others turn to alcohol, drugs, shopping, an affair, work, pornography, the internet, food, anything to take our minds off our suffering. We know this is a dangerous choice, but as Sheila wondered in the beginning of this chapter, death or arrest might be better than what we are facing now.

If you can relate to any of this, you are not alone. You are not the only person feeling this way. You are not the only person to fantasize about walking away from all of it, or even imagining something awful happening to those you love. These are dark admissions to make, but your honesty is an important part of moving forward.

It is likely difficult for you to find people to talk to. Maybe you have tried a support group for people who are experiencing similar things. You can google support groups for cancer caregivers, senior caregivers, or parents of special needs kids.

These groups mostly offer emotional support and empathy, and that is important. They may also teach specific coping skills or list local resources. These are also very important. But we might still feel something is missing.

I came to understand support groups after my wife and I adopted our son out of the foster care system. We met biweekly with other parents who struggled with the new children in their homes. There were behavior issues and attitude adjustments (the former the children, the latter the parents, although the lines were frequently blurred in both directions). There were horror stories and war wounds. We understood each other deeply, especially when one or more of us were overwhelmed. There was no judgment. We offered lifelines to each other when we could. Or, if there was no solution, we jumped into the emotional whirlpool with our friend and treaded water next to them, even if they were going down for the third time.

This book was born from another support group, this one for the parents of children with fetal alcohol spectrum disorder (FASD). Our son was exposed to alcohol in utero. He has FASD. This is a common lifelong neurobehavioral condition that can cause many physical and brain-based problems throughout life. Many people think of FASD as just causing facial features, like a flat nose or slanted eyes, but that actually occurs in less than 10 percent of people with this condition. The more challenging effects are difficulty with emotional regulation, executive functioning, learning problems, social difficulties, language processing, and uneven development called dysmaturity.

Many of these children are diagnosed with attention deficit hyperactivity disorder (ADHD), autism, mood disorders, and if adopted, reactive attachment disorder. However, a more fundamental challenge specific to FASD is a poorly developed corpus collosum, which helps the right and left brain communicate. This makes seeing the big picture and connecting ideas difficult. It can also make it harder to understand cause and effect. Memory, especially working memory, can be significantly impaired.

As a result, a child with FASD who has also experienced the trauma of parental neglect, abuse, or separation can have many challenging behaviors. Some of these children can be violent. Parenting a child with FASD requires a total change in perspective on how to parent. One can feel defeated, lonely, and exhausted, and sometimes unsafe. My wife and I felt all these things, and we joined an online forum to talk about them.

Late one night I was reading a post from a mother of another child with fetal alcohol spectrum disorder. She was at her wit's end, following weeks of struggle. Her son was raging, had been arrested and released and was now back home. He was failing at school, had no meaningful friendships and was blaming her for everything. She was recounting all the "professionals" whose services she had enlisted in the past several months. She was bemoaning the fact that none of the professionals seemed to understand what she was going through.

At first, I felt guilty because she was clearly suffering, and I did not have any extra care to give. Others in the group were offering to come over, they were calling her. I did not have the energy to do that. I knew I was tapped out. This was growth for me: I knew my limit. But still, I felt terrible. There was so much unmet need in my son, in me, in my community.

In the middle of her post, this woman had written, "I wish I could sleep through the night. I wish there were pastors and rabbis who understood FASD. I wish there were people who could take my kid to the movies for a few hours . . ." The list went on, but my eyes had fallen on the second wish.

"I wish there were pastors and rabbis who understood FASD."

Well. There was something I might be able to do. I am a pastor who understands FASD. And I know how hard it is to talk to a pastor who doesn't understand FASD, when they suggest stronger discipline or setting boundaries or taking breaks from the kids which are not as easy to do with FASD kids as with healthy children. And God help us when the only advice they have is to "pray harder."

A large percentage of foster and adoptive parents are people of faith. Their faith shapes their home life and inspires them to invite a child into their home. Their faith motivates them and sustains them during the difficult times. Some consider foster care a way to offer Christ's love in the world. Some might say, "I can love this child because God has always loved me, in spite of my flaws." So, faith is one resource for those of us with difficult home lives.

Generally speaking, if you foster-adopt from a government agency, your family is provided with therapists, medical doctors, educational support, and a social worker. There may also be "wraparound services" that offer parent partners, who are parents who are part of the foster care system and can provide empathy and wisdom; behavioral specialists, who work to change specific behaviors of the child; psychiatrists to administer medications; and tutors to help with educational issues. Our son came with a court-assigned special advocate (CASA), who helps foster children navigate the multiple court, educational, and county systems. He also had a lawyer to represent him in the multiple court appearances he had had over the years. These are not court appearances for infractions *he* had committed. They are court appearances where a judge gets to say every six months that his birth parents are not fit to care for him. Children leave that awful experience with a new stuffed animal and more feelings than I can imagine.

In the first five years he was with us, our son had three dentists, six doctors, five therapists, and five social workers, most of whom only needed to see him once or twice to interview him for the specific parts of his case on which they worked. Before we adopted him, we had to keep a log of every appointment he had in a month, including extracurricular activities and family visits. It was a lot of work, physically exhausting and emotionally draining.

Of course, foster-adopt parents are not the only caregivers whose reservoirs are depleted. The "sandwich generation" is made up of adults who are sandwiched in the middle of caring for their school-aged children and their ailing parents. While their children are moving toward independence, their parents are becoming more dependent. These caregivers get very little relief and are overwhelmed by the constant change in behavior and relationships at both ends of the family spectrum. Spouses who must care for their ailing husbands or wives must manage the special needs of their loved one while experiencing the loss of their soulmate. The loneliness can be devastating, but there are so many doctor appointments and physical problems or cognitive losses to adjust to that the caregivers rarely get the attention *they* need. That marital promise "for better and for worse" rings in the caregivers' ears, or they choke on the words each day.

In our case there were people trying to manage our son's physical, mental, educational, occupational, and legal issues. But no one cared for his soul, nor ours. We needed spiritual care, not because we are people of faith, but because we are humans. While we needed all the practical help being offered, we needed something deeper. I would argue we all do. Much of the struggle in our world, from war to global conflict to arguments in the US Congress, may have a spiritual aspect. I am not suggesting a quick solution like, "We all need Jesus." This is to say our souls are aching and it comes out in terrible, destructive ways. We have so many unmet needs, and there is not enough money and food in the world to fill some of the holes in our lives. We are not whole unless our souls are also cared for.

A spiritual need, or a damaged spirit, may feel like an itch that cannot be scratched. It may feel like listlessness. It may feel like resentment or loss of purpose. It usually feels like being misunderstood. If we are in touch with our soul or our spirit on a regular basis, hopefully we can tell when it's being depleted. If we do not have a real sense of our own spirit, we do not recognize the feeling of it being unhealthy. We just know we are out of balance. We can have a hundred reasons why, all of them accurate. We are not getting enough sleep, we are fighting with our family, our boss doesn't understand us. Money is tight, shifts are longer, our back went out. All these things may be true, but we know, deep down inside, that even if all these problems were solved, there would still be something wrong. We have a tug, not really in our hearts, not really in our stomachs, somewhere much deeper and more mysterious than that, telling us there must be something more. There must be a connection we are missing. That's our soul, crying out in the darkness, asking to be filled.

For some, religious communities help fill this need. But religious communities are filled with people with their own problems and are not always patient with the disruptions of hyperactive children or disruptive adults. Pastors and rabbis are rarely trained in this type of intervention. And few of us have found helpful spiritual words to offer, besides "God bless you," or "I am praying for you." I appreciate those words a lot. But they are rarely enough. We need honesty. We need to be able to scream at God and trust God will stay by us. We need hope when we are hopeless, but we also need good-hearted people to sit with us while we shake our fists at God. There are no simple answers to any of these problems, and I join you in resenting anyone who suggests there are. I promise I will never say, "You just need to have faith." Those words never work for me, and I doubt they work for you.

I offer this book to address the spiritual needs of caregivers. Parents of high-needs children, children of seniors who are facing end-of-life health issues, hospital staff, therapists, pastors; much is required of us. Most of us know we need to take care of ourselves, but this is a very difficult challenge, given the demands of our time and our mental capacities. How often do we say, "I cannot add one more thing to my plate." The idea of caring for our soul sounds great in theory, but who has the time?

I see you. I hear you. I am one of you. I am a middle-aged, highly educated white woman. I am an ordained pastor in the Evangelical Lutheran Church in America. I am a Lutheran because our founder,

Martin Luther understood that the human experience was *tough*, and God does not provide easy answers. Lutherans cling to the promises of God found in the Bible, but we also believe in science, psychology, and the human experience. I believe God loves us but does not swoop in and make everything right. I also believe there are a lot of different paths to God, or the sacred, or nirvana, or whatever concept makes sense for you. While this book is written mostly from the Judeo-Christian perspective, I hope those who cannot believe directly in God may find some comfort and helpfulness in these pages.

Each chapter addresses a different spiritual need. Perhaps this book will be helpful if read and ingested in its entirety. Perhaps it will be helpful to turn to a chapter as a spiritual need comes up in your life. Your goal may be to get closer to God or at least to transcend from this earthly struggle. Your goal may be to tend to your spirit. Your goal may be to try to *find* your spirit, buried under the piles of other things you are worrying about. There are many, many paths you may take to feed your soul. But you only have one soul, and you need it to be full.

You deserve this. As Pierre Teilhard de Chardin said, "We are not human beings having a spiritual experience. We are spiritual beings having a human experience." You have heard lots of advice about how to care for your body or your mind or your relationships. Let's take some time caring for your soul.

CHAPTER ONE

Chaos

In the beginning, when God created the heavens and the earth,
the earth was a formless void
and darkness covered the face of the deep,
while the spirit of God swept over the face of the waters.
Then God said, "Let there be light";
And there was light.
And God saw that the light was good;
and God separated the light from the darkness.
God called the light Day
and the darkness he called Night.
And there was evening and there was morning,
the first day.

—Genesis 1:1–5

Our family had barely gotten through the holidays. This is not unusual in stressed families. It is not unusual in foster homes. Many of us have unrealistic expectations of how the holidays should be. Some of us are still trying to forget painful holiday memories, or we are trying to recreate an idyllic memory from decades earlier which may or may not be based in reality. There may be so much disappointment, so many unmet needs. There may be miscommunications or a forced family meal with people who do not care for each other or are outright dangerous to each other. Some families just keep trying. Others finally agree to stop trying and spend holidays apart.

Our son has an especially hard time during the holidays, as many foster children do. His birthday, also a triggering event for many foster kids, is in November, just as the holiday season begins. Our first birthday and holiday season with him in our home had not gone well. He felt terrible, we felt terrible. We were still learning how to navigate difficult feelings and bad reactions. I do not want to go into details, but let's just say one night our family had to leave a restaurant before the food came, and once in the car I screamed at him with so much venom I barely recognized myself. We had enough hurt feelings and shame to go around for weeks. Our foster support team started to talk seriously with us about removing our son from our home. My wife and I often name this exact moment as a key turning point in our family. We could have said no to him at that point and felt justified. But somehow, we agreed to keep going. Call it grit, call it stupidity, call it love, we kept going.

We agreed to keep him in our home, but instead of feeling better about making a decision, I felt more unsettled. My feet had been swept out from underneath me. I had taken in a lot of emotional salt water. I was drowning.

I was in a crisis of faith. Like so many overwhelmed caregivers, I was not sure where I was or what God was doing. I met with my spiritual director, who is something of a combination pastor/counselor/therapist for pastors and others seeking to deepen their spiritual life. I was exhausted and terrified as I described the events of the past three months. I was unrecognizable to myself. Who was this basket case of nerves and anger? I couldn't hold my tongue. I couldn't calm down. I don't remember which one of us finally named what was going on in my family, but it was definitely the right word: *chaos*.

Total, utter chaos.

I could picture what this chaos looked like. It was a maelstrom, a whirlpool of color and wind and heat. There was steam or smoke coming from it. It was like lava, hot and ever-changing. It seemed dangerous. Frightening. No living creature would venture into it.

"Where is God in this chaos?" asked my spiritual director.

The verses from Genesis 1 came immediately to mind. "The spirit of God hovered over the waters." And so, I answered without thinking first:

"God is hovering over the chaos . . . about to create something new."

While that is a nice little Sunday School answer, there was a lot of metaphor at work. Whether you believe the creation story as a literal interpretation of the first moments of the cosmos or see it as a myth to explain how we came to be, those first verses of Genesis have some fruit to give us.

What existed before anything existed? *The Jewish Study Bible* makes this comment:

> To modern people, the opposite of the created order is "nothing," that is, a vacuum. To the ancients, the opposite of the created order was something much worse than "nothing." It was an active, malevolent force we can best term "chaos." In this verse, chaos is envisioned as a dark, undifferentiated mass of water. (Oxford University Press, 2004, p. 13, n. 2)

"Something much worse than 'nothing.'" Some people refer to it as the "formless void." Others call it "chaos."

Yup. My family life was not, and is not, "a nothing." "An active, malevolent force" sounds closer to the truth. Boiling, swirling, dangerous: those words are more accurate descriptors. A violent eddy of chaos and I was barely treading water in it.

Now I was imagining the spirit of God hovering above the chaos, just about to make sense of it all. In the biblical story, God looks at that chaos and creates light. And God saw that it was good.

Martin Luther King Jr. famously said, "Darkness cannot drive out darkness. Only light can do that." But in this creation story, light does not drive out darkness; light *comes* from darkness. I would suggest *only God* is capable of such a thing. How can something that is the *exact opposite* of the other thing be created? It's a miracle.

And so, in my chaotic family, the exact opposite might be in the process of being formed. After the chaos comes order. After conflict comes trust. Is it possible?

Let's go back to the creation story.

God said, "Let there be light"; and there was light.

Does anybody else think it's great that *the first thing* we need when things are being created is light? We must expose truths. We must see what we are working with. We need to understand the place, the limitations, the possibilities. Every good workbench has a strong lamp over it. The only way to start something new is to shine a light on the situation and assess what needs to be done.

God saw that the light was good; and God separated the light from the darkness.

Notice the darkness does not go away. It becomes differentiated. There will be light, and there will be darkness.

God called the light Day, and the darkness he called Night.

Not only does God allow both things to exist, but God gives darkness a name, "Night." Naming something always gives it value. God believes darkness has enough merit that it should be given a name. And a place. And a regular opportunity to be present. It makes one think God finds the darkness necessary. Maybe even *helpful*. This first division of light and dark may be considered God creating order; God is breaking the chaos into manageable, reliable chunks. We can expect darkness (and the subsequent sunrise) on a regular basis. Even the creation story tells us chaos is always close at hand. But so is a new day.

God can create amazing beauty from this chaos. God can create order and reason and things that can be expected. Things that can be counted upon. Also: chaos is not sustainable. Even a screaming child wears herself out at some point. Family arguments may seem interminable, but people do leave the room. Or the state. Or they die. No human can stay at a crisis point indefinitely.

But the last sentence of the creation story may be its most beautiful, and its most overlooked.

There was evening and there was morning, the first day.

The first day of our world.

The first full expression of "being" a universe.

The first time period into which all our hopes and dreams and activities will be counted. A day.

The first meaningful, ordered *thing* of the universe was a day. And it could only come to being because there was both darkness and light.

It might be best to stop this chapter here. God gets all the credit for ordering the chaos in these first pages. That is way it should be. We need to realize we need a higher power than ourselves to keep from swirling downward. We cannot save ourselves; we need help.

And yet . . .

There are a few other observations I want to make about this very helpful image of the maelstrom swirling about. Whirlpools move in one direction. Everything in that whirlpool has to move in the same direction. When I was young, my family had a "doughboy" pool. It was about a twelve-foot round metal-sided pool, constructed above ground, with a rubber lining that was filled with water. The pool was only about three feet deep, so we kids could stand up everywhere in the pool. One of our favorite things to do was to walk around the perimeter of the pool, circling the pool over and over and over, creating a whirlpool. Even though we were young children, after several minutes there would be a strong current running around the pool.

Now we could lift our feet and let the whirlpool whip us around the perimeter. If it started to slow down, all we had to do was start running around the edge of the pool again and reenergize the maelstrom.

Everything in the pool moved in the same direction, people, floats, goggles, leaves. There was no escaping the spinning. If we tried to move against the current, we would quickly lose strength, fall over, and get swept away.

Even though chaos in our homes feels like we are being blown in multiple directions, I think families are caught up in a current that moves us in the same, destructive path. The only way to break this motion is to get out of the pool. Even the children who *wanted* to make a whirlpool were dismayed to realize they could not stop what they had started. They simply had to get out for a while and let the waters calm down.

Disengagement may be the answer. In every story of chaos in our family, if only one of us had stepped away from the argument, there would have been a different outcome. As soon as one person calms down, the entire system shifts. There is nothing to react against. Most of us realize the destructive patterns of arguing and blame and abuse continue because all parties remain too engaged in the maelstrom. Taking a break may be all that is necessary to reset the situation.

We would love to point fingers at this point and say, "Yes! He needs to stop what he is doing, and I can calm down!" or "It's all her fault, she makes me so mad!" These things may be true. But we cannot control the other person. We may not even be able to control our emotional reaction. But we can control what we *do* after having emotions. We can take a break. We can keep our mouth shut. We can say something noncommittal like, "You might be right." The person *may* think we are agreeing, when we are only saying there is a possibility the person is right. We are not actually acquiescing.

This strategy only works when there are two functioning adults in this argument. If a person is disabled, they may not be physically able to step away. If a person is mentally disabled, they may not be capable of being fully present to participate in keeping their mouth shut or responding appropriately.

This idea of *not* engaging in the argument is hard for many of us. We believe if we just keep talking, someday we will come up with the right argument and convince our difficult person they were wrong. But let me ask you something: How has that worked so far? Have you ever convinced the person with whom you are in this infernal chaos that they are wrong, and you are right? Probably not. Tell me again why you keep trying?

Oh, it's painful, this dropping the fight. But so is staying in the chaos. So is this drowning. What if you stopped kicking against the tide and just relaxed? Will you die? Or would you be moved to a different place in the maelstrom and possibly find a toe hold? If you stopped flailing, might you see someone or something reaching out to help you?

Are you part of the problem? Have you ever been the one to start the fight? Or, maybe more likely, are you so damaged and "on edge" that you overreact to the slightest provocation? I hate admitting that about myself. I look back on *so many fights* and see the other person may have been asking a simple question. They may have just come in at the wrong moment. I may have been on a hair trigger, and they set me off for no reason. Or they are the reason I am tense, but they had not done anything to deserve the tirade I unleashed. What if we did not take the bait? What if we realized we were too triggered and stepped away? What if we did not react the way we *always* react and see how the other person responds? They may keep pushing, to get the reaction they also depend upon. They may escalate. And perhaps you can handle it. Or perhaps you can begin to see the truth of the chaos in which you live.

Recently, I felt *completely* justified in flipping my lid. People had done things they should not have done, they said things they should not have said, and *I needed them to understand how bad it was*. I kept a call log to make sure I had called every single person who Needed to Understand. Six calls in seven minutes. Lots of angry voicemails. I was on fire. I quickly texted my coach so she could see how efficient I was: "Look at how much I'm getting done to shut this thing down!" I wrote.

You know what she said in response? You might expect, "Way to take the lead!" Or, "Now they will understand!" Instead, she suggested I should look at why I was so reactive. I was looking for justification from my coach but instead got a teachable moment. I was not pleased. I am still not pleased, but I hope if I write this down, I will start to see the error of my ways. I overreacted. I created the chaos. A problem had arisen, but I made it significantly worse by stirring the pot, by jumping in the pool and running around the perimeter until I had a good ol' whirlpool going.

The Jewish Study Bible calls the chaos of Genesis 1 the "formless void." Chaos is "envisioned as a dark, undifferentiated mass of water."

A dark, undifferentiated mass: there's a new insult to hurl at someone. But I wish to focus on the "undifferentiated" part of that phrase. We may tend to think of "chaos" as something that has a lot of moving parts. But maybe chaos should be thought of as a bag of fighting cats. We see movement in there, but we cannot really tell where one cat ends and the next one begins. Part of the chaos is the lack of definition. Think of the "blob" from the 1950s horror movie: an undefinable mass of destruction that swallows up everything in its path, leaving no sign of people, animals, plants. All identity is lost when the blob rolls along.

Perhaps the chaos could have been managed if each participant in the maelstrom knew their true identity. Imagine if I had taken time to see who I was in this crisis, rather than jumping right into the maelstrom and losing myself. There are individuals with feelings and motivations and opinions working here, not just "a family in crisis." As the mental health professionals suggest: be curious about why the person is reacting the way they are. Be curious about why *you* are reacting the way you are. Come with compassion, including compassion for yourself. Why are people acting this way?

This is extraordinarily difficult to do when one or more of the people in the maelstrom do not have the tools to articulate their purpose. If you are dealing with a young child, or a mentally ill person, or a disabled senior, it may be close to impossible to figure out what is really going on. But you *can* figure out what is really going on with you. Are you really just tired, or hungry, or angry that you have been interrupted? Are you scared that your mother *cannot* understand how sick she is? Are you frustrated that your child *will never* take responsibility for himself? Is this fight *really* about what you think it is about?

It is incredibly difficult to determine what the fight is about *while you're in the fight*. So, give yourself a break if you do not know why you are so angry. You are in fight or flight mode. Why should we expect you to also be introspective?

Think about our young swimmers. If a child wished to get out of the pool, they climbed out and could watch the others swirl past. They could rest. They could put on shoes to strengthen their grip against the torrent. They could watch the whirlpool go by and figure out where they wanted to get back in, either near another swimmer or next to the pool float. You get the idea. Once out of the pool, a kid had the chance of entering back into the whirlpool with new strength, or a new plan.

Of course, the kid also has the option to not get back into the whirlpool. Some of us have the privilege of making that kind of choice. Others do not. And let's be honest: some of us like the feeling of the whirlpool and would happily jump back in and swirl around to the point of exhaustion.

So now might be a good time to step out of the maelstrom and self-assess. Are you responsible for stirring up the water? Are you simply floating along, banging into everything? Are you desperately trying to get your feet to touch the ground so you can stabilize? Are you walking against the current? Are you trying to get out of the pool, or are you joyfully jumping back in?

You may be a participant in the chaos, and you need to understand that.

But there is also God.

Just like in the Genesis story, a loving God is there too, wishing to make something new out of this chaotic mess. Just like "in the beginning," God is longing to make light come from this formless void.

This may be the point upon which to meditate. What might God be doing in this chaos? Do not allow yourself to think that God is punishing you. Do not think God is twisting you around for the sport of it. We understand people are broken. To be human is to have hurts. And to be hurt is to hurt others. We do this to ourselves, either on purpose or by accident of birth. There are many theories as to why this is true, from original sin to human nature to early trauma to greed to survival instinct. We are hurt, so we hurt others.

Now ask yourself, where is God in this chaos? What does God want to do in the whirlpool? What might God do when we are drowning? What mighty thing does God do when we are out of options?

There are several stories in the Bible where Jesus's disciples are out on their boat in the middle of the night. Jesus has stayed behind to pray, and there is no plan on how they will reunite on the other side of the water. One night, as described in Matthew 14, Jesus comes walking across the water, either to join them, or just to get to the other side, and the disciples spy him from a distance. They are reasonably freaked out about seeing some human figure walking toward them, until they see it is their teacher and friend. Now Peter, the One with the Big Ideas, asks if he can come out on the water too. As soon as he steps out from the boat, he apparently starts to walk. Wow. Maybe it is going to be okay, Peter's moving into some sort of Supernatural Big League. But, as the story goes, Peter immediately gets distracted by the wind and the waves, *the chaos*, and starts to sink. The next part of the story is remarkable (as if the other parts were not fantastic and fantastical). Jesus, who is still standing on top of the water, reaches down and pulls Peter up, lifting him back into the boat. The physics of this are impossible. Okay, the physics of the entire story are impossible. But think of it, Jesus *in the middle of a windstorm*, while standing on top of water, lifts a grown man out of the water and saves him. "With God, all things are possible," Jesus promises in Matthew 17. That "all things" piece applies to your chaotic life too.

You are a beautiful swimmer in God's eyes. God adores you, the playful child who wanted to make a whirlpool in the pool and then had to deal with the consequences. Or perhaps you were born in this swirl, inheriting a lot of chaos through no fault of your own. Now, imagine: Where is God? A lifeguard at the side of the pool, making sure you remain safe? The buoy you are clinging to? A strong swimmer coming from the opposite direction to save you? Maybe God is floating next to you, cheering you on, warning you against dangers. God wants to protect us when life gets difficult, even if it is our doing that creates the chaos, or we cannot pull ourselves out of a chaos we inherited.

God can create something beautiful out of utter chaos. We have seen this over and over again, in our biblical stories, in our own stories. We see it in the renewal of nature. We see it when life comes after death. God can do remarkable, creative, regenerative things. Consider what those things might be. Even in your chaotic life. Especially in your chaotic life.

What does God want to do with the chaos?

CHAPTER TWO

Loss of Home

By the rivers of Babylon—
    there we sat down and there we wept
    when we remembered Zion.
On the willows there we hung up our harps.
For there our captors asked us for songs,
and our tormentors asked for mirth, saying,
    "Sing us one of the songs of Zion!"

How could we sing the Lord's song in a foreign land?
If I forget you, O Jerusalem,
    let my right hand wither!
Let my tongue cling to the roof of my mouth,
    if I do not remember you,
if I do not set Jerusalem
    above my highest joy.

Remember, O Lord against the Edomites
    the day of Jerusalem's fall,
how they said, "Tear it down! Tear it down!
    Down to its foundations!"
O daughter of Babylon, you devastator!

> Happy shall they be who pay you back
> what you have done to us!
> Happy shall they be who take your little ones
> and dash them against the rock!
>
> —Psalm 137

This psalm was written by the people of Judah (part of ancient Israel) as they sat in exile, having been taken from their homeland by invading Babylonians. It is a pivotal chapter in the story of God's people. The Old Testament, or Hebrew Bible, has plenty of stories of the people of Israel and their successes: Abraham becomes the father of all religion, Moses leads the people out of Egypt to the promised land. King David and his armies destroy their enemies. King Solomon takes advantage of a time of peace to build beautiful cities and a temple for God. Things were looking good.

But the Bible also has plenty of stories of disobedience and consequence. King Solomon starts marrying the local girls. Girls with other customs and other gods. So, Solomon started worshipping some of those gods. Maybe it started slowly, praying to a local god to amuse one of his conquests. Then perhaps he built a shrine to another god, partly to impress a woman, partly to prove he could do whatever he wanted. At some point, the scales tipped, and Solomon was moving away from Israel's God to the idols of his neighbors and wives.

After Solomon died, many of the future kings "did evil in the sight of the Lord," as the Bible recounts. They became less and less obedient or responsive to the word of God. So, as a consequence, God favors their enemies, and Israel is overrun by the Babylonians.

This psalm, then, is written from a place of devastation. God has punished the people by letting Babylon (and Assyria, who conquered the northern territories of Israel) conquer them.

The exiles are seated by the river of Babylon. They are remembering their homeland, here referred to as Zion. Their captors are forcing them to sing songs from home, but the people are too heartbroken to mutter the tune.

The psalmist is miserable. Sitting in the dirt. Remembering home, a place long-gone and destroyed. This is a basic, terrible human truth. Many of us long for home, even if we are still living in a childhood house. We lose home in a variety of ways.

In the book *The Primal Wound* (1993), Nancy Verrier talks about the loss a child feels when removed from their mother, called the "primal wound" even if it is at birth. The child may have no other contact with their birth mother, but there is a deep connection to the person who has given birth to them. We grieve losing our mothers, even if we are never with them once we leave the womb. Tragically, the primal wound affects how we connect to people and understand relationships for the rest of our lives. This does not mean adopted people cannot be happy; they can. They can lead vital, full lives. But many of them suffer from a deep longing that they can barely explain. They are sitting on the shore in Babylon. They are not home.

I also think about our senior citizens placed in facilities, or our hospitalized mentally ill, or those who are in long-term institutional rehabilitation after illness or injury. Their new "home away from home" may be beautiful. It may have caring staff and restorative environments. But it is not home. The loss felt is existential, emotional, mental, and spiritual. Place matters.

Refugees long for their home country, foster children and orphans long for their parents. The hospitalized long for their bed, the widower longs for the way his life used to be.

Back to the psalm: The description of Babylon is quite beautiful. They are seated at a river with willow trees. They are being asked to play music, the music of their homeland. This may be some people's picture of what heaven looks like, yet the psalmist is despondent. Babylon is not his home.

And it never will be.

There is an interesting dilemma in this psalm, one that may not be considered in a quick reading:

If I forget you, O Jerusalem,
Let my right hand wither!

> Let my tongue cling to the roof of my mouth
> if I do not remember you,
> if I do not set Jerusalem above my highest joy.

There is a sense of loyalty here that must be admired. If the author ever forgets his homeland, he prays for his right hand to wither. He would rather be deformed than lose his commitment to his birthplace. He wants his tongue to cling to the roof of his mouth, so he can not eat or drink, should he forget from whence he came. This is a serious statement.

Imagine what it must be like for a foster or adopted child to start to attach to a new family and a new home. She may finally begin to relax, finally begin to hope, but also hates herself for "forgetting Jerusalem," that is, forgetting her birth family. Foster children have been known to act out after having a particularly good period with foster families. There are very complicated feelings about a new place. And enormous ambivalence and pain in letting go of dreams of returning home.

To be honest, the last part of this psalm is often omitted in devotionals and sermons:

> Happy shall they be who pay you back
> what you have done to us!
> Happy shall they be who take your little ones
> and dash them against the rock!

This is among the most violent language found in the Bible. The author is dreaming of a horrific act of revenge, in which the children of their oppressors are killed. You can see why pastors are hesitant to read this aloud on a Sunday morning.

And yet it is helpful to have these verses here. They remind us how deep the feelings of anger and hatred and revenge are when we are removed from our home. We hope those who took away our home feel as bad as we do, if not worse. We also hope their future is destroyed, as we are sure ours is.

This psalm does not just describe the losses felt by those who are sick or lost or abandoned. This psalm *also* describes the pain of caregivers who have also lost their home, *even if they are still living in it.*

Foster and adoptive parents are, by definition, people of great hope and vision. They believe they have built a home and a family with enough love to go around. They want to share this home with strangers, children they wish to make their own. They have fantasies about what that family will look like: grateful children, healing after years of unhappiness in their abusive home or multiple failed placements, lovingly and willingly engaging in a family life that looks just like the idyllic childhood the parents had. Or the adoptive parents hope this new family will be the direct opposite of the home life *they* suffered through when they were young. This new family will be different, better, healthier than the nightmare of their own upbringing. Their home will be like a river: calm and refreshing, bringing life and vibrancy to all who sit lazily on her shores. There will be times of music and community, of integrity and newly minted memories.

But the children come into the home, and nothing is as the parents had planned. The children might hate the food placed in front of them, they may destroy the toys they have been given, some sulk in their rooms or scream at their well-meaning parents. In the worst case, some get in trouble at school or are chronically truant, others get arrested, hit their siblings, torture the cat. There are a lot of emotions, and it never lets up.

The parents cry out for their Jerusalem, the holy city, of their dreams. Or they long for the peaceful home they had before they welcomed children into it. Many placements fail once the parents get to this Babylonian river moment, when they cry out for a home that once was, or that they had dreamed of. They feel the *children* are the parents' *captors*, and if the parents do not surround themselves with support, they will rail against the helplessness of their imprisonment until they end their misery with a call to the social worker to "take this brat out of here."

Caregivers for debilitated patients, such as elders or the chronically ill, and especially if these patients are family members, may also grieve the Jerusalem they once knew. They remember a time *before* hospital beds in the living room and on-call nurses and IV bags and the chair in the shower. They remember a time when their spouse could still carry on a conversation with them. They remember a time when they didn't have to perform the most basic functions for their loved one, from feeding to dressing to helping with toileting or changing diapers. There is rarely a beautiful river flowing through this type of intensive caregiving. There is rarely a time for music and reminiscing. The reminiscing is sometimes too painful because it reminds the family of a relationship they will never see again.

Those living with addicts and the mentally ill agonize over the home they once had or fooled themselves into believing existed at one point. As the first step of Al-Anon and Alcoholics Anonymous states, "We came to admit our lives had become unmanageable." Everything feels out of control. The ground shifts beneath our feet. We cannot depend on anything, not a schedule, not an appropriate response from our loved ones. Our home, real or imagined, is gone.

If you can relate to this, you must recognize you are grieving the Jerusalem you once knew, even if that Jerusalem was always a fantasy. See if you had unicorns and fairy dust somewhere in your mind's eye. That's always an indicator that you were hoping for an unrealistic home life. Of course, I am kidding about the fairy dust, but if you dreamt of grateful children who were obedient and loving, you were setting yourself up. Ask your friends with biological children how often *they* are grateful and loving. If you were hoping when your dad moved into your home that you'd *finally* have a satisfying relationship with him, you may have been hoping for something that will never be possible. Again, I quote the Al-Anon goals which strive to have a life of contentment *whether or not the addict stops using*. We are longing to find our home, whether or not the one we love changes or is cured.

It is time for a serious self-assessment: Would you rather be crippled by your fantasies (or your memories of how it once was) or would you rather figure out how to live the fullest life possible, now that you reside in Babylon?

Did I mention the first important step is to honestly express your disappointment about the loss of your home? You need to talk about it, write about it, punch pillows, take up jogging, sing your head off, break pencils, do anything you can to feel it deeply.

Do not feel guilty about resenting your Babylon. Join the millions of unhappy people who want to shout, "Someone has made a mistake! I don't belong here!" You were supposed to be living in Jerusalem! Of course, you hate this place, even though it does have a river and some nice trees. They are not the trees you are used to.

You need to feel the feelings, and express them, but you must be thoughtful about who gets this tirade. Our children, our sick, our elderly do not truly understand what a prison they have built in our lives. Most of them would *never* want to be responsible for this type of agony.

It is also not fair to dump on our co-parent, or spouse, or sibling who is also caring for Mom or Dad. They're probably having as much trouble holding up as we are. We cannot be each other's therapists. It would be a time saver, it would be cheaper financially, but the emotional cost is too high for everyone. We must avoid dumping on each other. This is a *very* difficult pact to maintain. Our co-caregivers often understand the struggle. We may have shorthand to describe the stressful situations in which we find ourselves. We may be sharing the same physical space. It is important to lean on each other and support each other, but we need to be careful to not take it out on each other.

We may feel especially alone when those closest to us do not understand our feelings. Some of the most isolating moments I have had are when those "in the trenches" with me are having a different reaction than I am. I feel crazy, like everyone else has moved on and I'm still stunned that this is my life. We will talk about that isolation in chapter 5.

We need to find someone on the outside; a friend, a therapist, a pastor or rabbi, a support group, another caregiver who has some idea what we are experiencing, and we need to talk to them. Online chat groups work, *especially* when we are feeling guilty and don't want to look anyone in the eye while whining about how hard it is. But I would recommend *you do* look someone in the eye. Because there is an amazing moment that comes when you say you hate this place in which you live and their gaze softens and they understand exactly what you are talking about, whether they say so or not. And I recommend you keep looking for that look in someone's eye until you find it. You'll recognize it, I promise.

I have to be honest: I've been in support groups with people I don't like, and I see that look in their eye and I get what I need. It can come from strangers. It can also come from lifelong friends whom you had no idea would understand.

And after you have come to truly acknowledge how painful this place is, it's time to make an assessment. Can you keep going? Sometimes you will decide you cannot. Often you will decide there is no other choice. But that's not true. There is *always* another choice. You may believe sending the child away is not an option. You may say putting Mom in a home is not an option. You may say changing the care plan is not an option. But there are *always* options. They are options you do not wish to take. In that case, agreeing to stay in this situation is a *choice*. You made a decision, you actually had a say in that, even if it doesn't feel like it. You've made a choice, even if it seems desperate or forced, to keep living in Babylon.

I do not say this to make you feel miserable. I say this to make you feel empowered. You have discovered yourself in Babylon, and you are not happy about it. But you have decided it is best to stay. You may *never* come to love Babylon. Why would you? It is not your home.

My own decisions to stay involved as a caregiver are difficult. I am using "decisions" in plural because we decide over and over if we can still do this difficult work. I often look back at critical junctures and see how I continue to say "yes" to our son. Sometimes I wonder if I have made the right decision, but I have to realize it over and over again: I was the one who made that decision. I have agreed to stay in Babylon.

In 2018 Paramount Pictures released *Instant Family*, an incredibly honest portrayal of a couple, played by Mark Wahlberg and

Rose Byrne, who welcome three foster children into their home. It is *rough*. The kids' behavior is extremely difficult and unexpected. One night the exhausted couple are lying in their bed, fantasizing about sending all the kids away.

"I hate them so much," Wahlberg's character says. His wife agrees. They are energized, angry, desperate to get rid of them. They make a plan to call the social worker and send the kids away. They lie together in silence for a moment, and one of them says, "We're never going to get rid of them," and the other says, "I know." They have made the decision. Again. They will stay in Babylon. They have sealed their fate, but they want to do it. I burst into tears watching that scene. I had lived that scene myself. Many, many times.

Okay, so for today, or this hour, or this minute, you make the choice to stick around. You will not forget Jerusalem, the home of your memory or your fantasy. That will be with you forever. Do not worry about forgetting it. It's in your DNA. But it's time to start finding the garden spots of Babylon, because you are in this for the long haul. Or at least for another twenty-four hours.

This is a good time to pray. Ask God, ask the universe, ask some elusive sacred thing like love or beauty: "Please show me a little of the beauty of this place." Beauty shows up in very small spaces. You may see it in the twinkle of recognition in the eye of a mute Alzheimer's patient when a certain song is played on the radio. You may see it in the woman who suffers from fibromyalgia who gets to laugh for a few minutes. Or in the family that rejoices because their traumatized eight-year-old reduced his nightly tantrums from two hours to forty-five minutes. We may never forget the joys of our long-lost home, but we may be able to find beauty, even in Babylon.

When you discover something beautiful, you may need to write it down. That way you can reread it during the darkest of nights. I have a "Favorite Moment of the Day" journal that helps me record the simplest of joys. You may need to tattoo it on your heart. You may need to celebrate beauty with a nice meal or a small gift to yourself. You may need to start a jar of pennies (or rocks or buttons or gum wrappers), and you put one in every time something beautiful happens. Hopefully the jar will have more reminders of beauty in it than you imagined was possible.

These are long, difficult times. There is no other way to describe it. But beauty exists everywhere. Those of us in Babylon have simply become very good at finding it. So, find those friends, other refugees from their former life, other travelers on this difficult path. Tell them the truth, cry, then laugh yourselves silly, and find the beauty. You can do this. You have been doing it. Take a breath, enjoy the sunset, find the beauty.

CHAPTER THREE

Guilt

Demands on a caregiver are high. Few of us ever feel like we are doing enough. Guilt may be a constant companion. I can name several sources or types of guilt in thirty seconds, without even trying:

Guilt for not doing enough
Guilt for doing too much
Guilt for feeling resentment
Guilt for wondering if somehow we contributed to the person's illness or injury
Guilt for actually contributing to the person's illness or injury
Guilt for not having the same illness our loved one has ("Why not me?" or survivor's guilt)
Guilt for not understanding enough about the conditions our loved one endures
Guilt for not taking care of other family members or ourselves
Guilt for not being able to be in two or three places at once
Guilt for needing sleep or food
Guilt for feeling guilty

I wrote all those as fast as I could type. Recognize any of these in your life?

At the end of the day, we feel woefully inadequate. When I became a parent, I thought that ubiquitous phrase, "I have no idea what I am doing" was just a funny overexaggeration parents said to bond with other parents.

Then I realized they were dead serious. Parents frequently have no idea what we are doing. Those little baby humans change so fast, confounding us at every turn. The same is true for caregivers of adults. Caregivers are frequently stumped. The miracle drug stops working, the routine shifts. A strategy that worked perfectly for two months is suddenly completely ineffective.

Let's keep going: the same is true in relationship dynamics. There is a reason they are called "dynamics" and not "stabilities." Our relationships are dynamic because we are dealing with lots of moving parts, namely people with moods and emotions and physical changes (see above, harrumph) and schedules. As my son describes it, "About once a month I get completely annoyed with people who I usually like." He has no explanation for it. He just hates them. This lasts for about a week. And just as quickly, he moves back into relationship with them. And by "them," I mean "us."

We are dealing with people who are messy and unpredictable. And through it all, we feel guilty because we cannot keep on top of everything. I blame this on the *myth of mastery*. Particularly in the western hemisphere, we believe we can work hard enough and practice long enough and study everything and achieve mastery over mind and body and nature. Then we are stunned when we are stumped. There must be another book we can read! Maybe if we increase our proteins we will be stronger! The secret to success is sleeping less and exercising more! The secret to success is sleeping more! Relax! Work harder! Pick any two.

Here's the thing: we mostly feel guilty because we think we are not good enough. We think there is something wrong with us. This feeling is deep, practically inherent, in a lot of us. There are *so many* contributors to our self-worth: love and trauma, lack and excess, bad luck and small victories. They imprint on us in the womb, from early childhood and into adulthood. Some of us spend a small fortune on therapy to work this out. Some of us drink or shop or make terrible relationship choices to help ourselves feel better. Some commit to work or church or the gym or any number of distractions, healthy and unhealthy, to make ourselves feel better.

The psalmist reminds us, "I am fearfully and wonderfully made" (Psalm 139). We all are. I will be taking a lifetime to let that in, but you are wonderfully made. You may be a hot mess, but you are still God's delight.

A few years ago I was complaining about myself to a colleague, and she finally said, "That's a terrible thing to say about my friend Brenda." I loved that response. We talk about ourselves in a way we would never talk about others. Let's try to break that cycle.

But in this cycle of self-doubt, self-loathing, or just general guilt, we have to wade our way through a lot of advice. People always have an opinion about our lives. The advice is often contradictory. This contributes to confusion and guilt. If only we followed the *other* advice, we would not be having the difficulties we are having now. I will tell you the two messages I receive most frequently from our therapist: (1) Work harder at maintaining order and structure. You need to take control of your home. (2) Do not work so hard at maintaining order and structure. You need to stop trying to take control.

Being overwhelmed is a wonderful contributor to guilt. We are exhausted and then feel guilty about being exhausted.

Most humans realize we are not responsible for natural disasters like hurricanes and earthquakes. It is a fairly disturbed person who believes they cause (or prevent) hurricanes. But most of us feel guilt for not being able to stop other natural occurrences, like terminal illness or diminished mental capacities. Somehow, we think we should be able to do something. Cancer is unfair; legal systems do not make sense.

Trying to make sense of such things is another version of this myth of mastery. Surely, we should be able to explain why one of us gets hit by a car and another does not. There must be a reason why the sweet two-year-old gets cancer and her cranky grandmother lives to one hundred. To understand why bad things happen to good people would be to understand one of the great mysteries of life. If only we could master these truths, we could conquer them. And if we could conquer them, we would not have all these complex, icky feelings that we feel guilty for having.

There are plenty of things we cannot do. We are only human. We cannot perform miracles. We cannot turn back the hands of time. We cannot be in three places at once. We cannot survive on three hours of sleep at night and one meal a day. These things are true. And no amount of guilt will suddenly make these things change.

Letting go is an enormous part of the caregiver's journey. It is long and painful. A huge part of this is participating in frequent reality checks. Which things can you be responsible for, and which things can you not? You may need another person to help you make this assessment. At the end of the day, the only thing you can be responsible for is yourself. (Another lesson I will be learning for the rest of my natural life.) You cannot make anyone do anything. OK, *maybe* you can make a small child do your bidding, but even that runs at about a 65 percent success rate.

Maybe one of the key things you feel guilty about is your limits. You cannot go twenty-four hours a day. Maybe you cannot do as much as you are doing now. You are wearing down and feel terrible about it. You do not need to feel guilty about this. *No one* can do it. You are not a superhuman mutant, the only one on the planet who is able to go and go and go and never stop. And yet, most of us feel guilty that we are not superhuman. We remember a time when we were capable of more. It may be a fantasy, but we cling to it.

Word Porn, a popular page on Facebook, posts words and their definitions throughout the week. I recently came upon this one:

> Hiraeth—a homesickness for a home to which you cannot return, a home which maybe never was; the nostalgia, the yearning, the grief for the lost places of your past.

Hiraeth is an unbelievable contributor to guilt. It's the nostalgia that will kill you. Nostalgia has such a positive connotation: we remember the good ol' days. There may have been a time of health and wealth and security. But nostalgia is not helpful. We cannot spend too much time in the past. Those days are gone. Grieve that, as hard as you need to. But you need to stay in the present. You live in the present, and you need to love yourself in the here and now.

God loves you in the here and now. God loves you in your imperfection. God delights in your personality and your body and your mind and your foibles. This may be hard for you to accept. You may have been told we all sin and fall short of the glory of God. This is true, we are a mess as a species. And God made us because God wanted to be in relationship with us. God is perfect, we are not. Can you let go of the need to be perfect just a little bit? Can you ask God to show you something delightful about yourself? Maybe God can send you a friend to remind you of that? Maybe a family pet wants to let you know you are amazing? Maybe the feel of the breeze on your face or the taste of a piece of fruit or a sunset can remind you of this rich, complicated, impossible, and beautiful life you possess?

Look, this is hard stuff. Anyone who wants to fight you about this needs to be checked. They do not know what you are going through. Only you and God truly know. You have survived every day to this point. You have been brave and strong and steadfast against impossible odds. Your successes look different from others' successes. Your shortcomings are different from anyone else's. This is not a competition, this is life, and you are living it, the gritty, difficult, glorious life.

Remember my colleague who chastised me for saying such horrible things about her friend Brenda? Can you imagine God also wants you to stop trashing God's beautiful child, you? No, seriously. God was just bragging about you to me this morning. God does not want you to feel guilty. God wants you to feel loved.

Imagine that. What does God think about you? God thinks you are fantastic. God might have an odd way of showing that, but that's God doing God's thing. Keep going, friend. And see if you can lighten any of your load. Some of that load is guilt, shame, and some other junk you do not deserve. Let it go. You've got enough on your plate.

CHAPTER FOUR

Loss of Self-Identity

Now as Jesus and his disciples went on their way, they entered a certain village, where a woman named Martha welcomed him into her home. She had a sister named Mary, who sat at the Lord's feet and listened to what he was saying. But Martha was distracted by her many tasks; so she came to Jesus and asked, "Lord do you not care that my sister has left me to do all the work by myself? Tell her then to help me." But the Lord answered her, "Martha, Martha, you are worried and distracted by many things; there is need of only thing. Mary has chosen the better part, which will not be taken away from her."

—Luke 10:38–42

The story of Martha and Mary is a famous one in Christian circles. These two sisters are the epitome of service and spirituality. Martha is heralded as one who rolls up her sleeves and gets the job done. If you refer to a person as a "Martha," you mean they work hard, are dependable and might have trouble saying "no." We want about a dozen "Marthas" in our congregations.

Mary, on the other hand, is sometimes seen as a slouch, sometimes seen as a saint. She chooses *not* to play hostess at this dinner party, but instead, sits obediently at Jesus's feet. When someone is referred to as a "Mary," it might be in praise of their spiritual practices, but it may also be a passive-aggressive way to suggest they should get off their duff and help out a little more.

This story came up in a women's retreat at my church. Some of the women tried to say Mary got it right and wanted to criticize the "worker bee," Martha. Not surprisingly, a few "Martha" types flew off the handle at this critique.

"We need Marthas!" they exclaimed. "Nothing gets done if everyone is a Mary!"

A timid woman in the back spoke up. "Yes, but the text says Mary has chosen the better part . . . you can't get around that. Jesus clearly prefers Mary."

"Jesus didn't tell Martha to stop, now, did he? He was still hungry! Still wanted a meal on the table!" came the reply. This was personal. Women who related to being Martha felt judged. This was a moment of self-justification. Or at least self-definition.

And that is why I include this passage here. Caregivers often struggle with their definitions of themselves. They have lost their sense of who they are outside of the work they do. At the core of this Bible story are two women who understand who they are. Martha defines herself by her work. This is not a bad thing. She is not to be criticized for that. Her work matters. Of course it does. We *need* workers to care for us, to feed us, to clean the house. Even if those workers are *us*, we know if we do not do the job, it is not getting done.

I am guessing the other members of their community *also* define Martha by her work. They have come to depend upon her and know what she is capable of. Certainly, Mary knows Martha will take care of the meal arrangements. Even if Mary does not help, there is an assumption that everything will be handled.

Now consider the life of a caregiver. Most new parents despair as their friendships change: childless friends often fall away. Suddenly they find themselves running in a circle of other new parents: moms from day care, dads who drop off their kids at baseball practice. But the old friendships might be lost. You have the "Parents" friend group and the "Singles" friend group. I am not sure I would appreciate being labeled in either.

It is usually worse for caregivers who are isolated. They used to volunteer, they used to have coffee with friends. Now they are home alone. So much of how we recognize ourselves is through the eyes of others. How do we know ourselves when so many of the people in our lives have changed or are gone?

Unfortunately, more than our external life has changed. Our social life changed because our inner life changed. Caregivers have to spend enormous amounts of time *thinking* about the care they give. And if they have any compassion at all, they spend enormous amounts of time *feeling* about the care they give. After a while, our whole idea of who we are as people has changed. Our definition of ourselves has been altered. Their inner voice may be saying things like: "I barely recognize myself anymore. I don't recognize the things that I say. I don't recognize the look on my face. I don't remember ever feeling this tired. I certainly didn't know this would be the marriage I was in (or the family I was a part of, or the parent I would be)."

It is a desperate moment when we realize we are no longer the person we once were.

Martha defines herself by her work. I wonder if she is surprised when the words come out of her mouth, "Lord, do you not care that my sister has left me to do all the work by myself? Tell her then to help me." Martha is not feeling empowered by her self-definition, she is feeling overwhelmed by it. She lashes out, airing the family laundry in front of guests. Martha looks exhausted at best, petty and vindictive at worst.

There are days when I want everyone to know how hard it is to be a mother. Maybe if I articulate my agony clearly enough, I will get help, sympathy, or even chocolate. Maybe I could find someone who would care. Maybe I cannot. It is likely that those who would empathize are too busy being parents themselves to have time to hear me whine. I wish there were a hotline to call and say, "Do you not care how hard this child is? Make *someone* come help me!"

Frequently when we lose our inner strength, we need to declare it more often. A confident athlete does not have to brag about his skill, his stats prove it. A well-balanced musician will play well but does not have to point out how well she is playing. A caregiver who is confident in how they are managing their charges rarely has to draw attention to the care plan. But when we lose sight of ourselves, when we are not sure if we are doing well, we tend to ruminate on it. Extroverts will need to talk about it. A lot. Introverts might prefer to keep silent, but their minds are spinning 24/7 about their doubts.

When things are tough at my neighbor's house, he calls frequently. If long periods of time go by without hearing from him, we know things are stable. When I asked him if that was accurate, he smiled and said, "Things were going well at home, so I didn't need to tell anyone."

If Martha was happy with her role and her self-definition, we probably would not have this story in the Bible.

I do not mean to be harping on Martha. I love Martha. I relate to Martha. Too much. But she is twisted up emotionally because of how she defines herself. She is a nose-to-the-grindstone kind of girl, hosting a stop-and-smell-the-roses kind of guest. Jesus wants us to follow the Way, the Truth, and the Life. That may be defined in different ways, but his followers understand this work is done with a heart and soul, not by punching clocks or making lists. This is why we hail Mary as "getting it right" and Martha as "getting it wrong."

But how do you think Mary defines herself? Does she think of herself as a philosopher or a spiritual disciple? Probably not. Some scholars like to point out the fact that Mary sits at Jesus's feet, a position that would normally be held by men only. Mary is a rebel. Mary is part of the first generation of female disciples. Her presence at Jesus's feet might be revolutionary. Does Mary define herself as a feminist? Probably not. Does Mary define herself as a slouch? Does anyone define themselves as a slouch? Mary does not speak. Is this because she is insolent, or because she does not need to engage in the argument? It is possible she is silent because she is content. She does not feel the need to explain herself.

This may not be helpful in the family dynamic. It is likely there was quite a blow-up between the two sisters after the guests had left. But Mary is silent in the written account. We might make some guesses about her inner life. Mary does not respond because she does not feel threatened, because she is self-assured. Her definition of herself is likely more complex, more well-rounded. For this reason, Mary's self-definition may be a better one on which we should focus.

Martha might define herself with one word: worker. Or maybe servant. Or even obedient. Dutiful. Mary would not be able to define herself with one word. Her favorite characteristics would be internal, not external. She's passionate or compassionate. She is a thinker, a listener. She probably got criticized as a child for being a dreamer. It is likely she has a rich internal life. It is likely her sister does not.

Fine, you think. What do these sisters have to do with *me?* I am busy. I am exhausted. I need to wash dishes and make a shopping list before I go to bed. Oops, I've been interrupted three times by people calling my name. Why are we reading about Martha and Mary?

We are talking about losing our self-identity. This is a huge problem for caregivers. We lost our sense of self when we became workers. Servants. Slaves. We may not have started this caregiving relationship with this type of self-definition. We may have entered into this care because we loved the person we care for. We probably still love them. But we have lost ourselves in the care. It is a crisis. A spiritual crisis.

I would suggest the crisis came when we were reduced to one descriptor. We are defined, by ourselves or by others, in only one way. Nurse. Mom. Provider. Our internal life, our soul, has been sucked out of us. When I use the word "soul," I'm thinking of that rich, diverse, beautiful, fascinating part of you that God imagined when God first imagined you.

What feelings come up when I refer to a beautiful, fascinating part of you? Does it make you cry? Do you get angry? Are you just numb? Is there a tiny bit of recognition and hope? That delicious soul, that beautiful unique part of you is still in there. It is probably buried under care and need and exhaustion. It might be caught underneath shame or fear or sorrow. But it is there. I promise.

Write down three words to describe yourself.

Now write down three words you think other people would write down to describe you. These words can be nouns or adjectives. Do it now, before reading ahead.

What words have you chosen? (Seriously, write them down now before you read more. This is not a test. You won't be in trouble for picking the words you picked. Write them down before you continue, or you'll miss some of the fun.)

What words have you chosen? Many people write down roles: mother, banker, coach. While these words are absolutely accurate to describe you, do you feel they define you? It makes a bit more sense if you used role-words on the list that *other* people would use. They may only know you in your role. They may not know the inner you.

Role-words are nouns. Adjectives, on the other hand, are descriptions. They get to the inner you. White people frequently care about our roles. "What do you do?" is a great conversation starter. But does it get to the true person? "Who are you?" might be a better question, but ick, it sounds so personal and invasive. So, we hide behind a role, and might get praise for it. Martha did.

But who are you? What words would you use to describe yourself?

When you write down adjectives you see how you really feel about yourself. That is when you start to understand the inner you, *and how you feel about that inner you*. If you write *brave, tired, warrior* I would guess there is some empathy, some pride and some sense that life is hard, but you are fighting a good fight. (But there's a fight . . . hmm . . .) If you write *mother, seamstress, organist* you might get a good sense of how you are defining yourself. These are worthwhile titles, and things to be proud of. But where are your passions and your fears? Where does your heart lie? Of course, if the list is filled with criticism—*angry, bitter, old*—you may quickly see that you are in a different kind of trouble.

The way you define yourself matters. Do you think Mary used "role words" to describe herself? Do you think Martha did?

When I feel my worst, the words I use to describe myself are not kind. Sometimes they echo words other people have used to describe me when they were being cruel. It might be helpful to think about the origin of the words you use to describe yourself. Were there people who called you those things? Do you believe them to be true because you have heard these words your whole life? Or are you hearing them now, over and over again, from loved ones?

You deserve love and support around those injuries, even if they are decades old. A loving gift to yourself would be to talk to clergy, a therapist, a trusted friend about the tapes that keep playing in your head and find out how to push "stop" on those negative messages.

I am also capable of being very hard on myself *without* a script from someone else. I can give you a list of things I do badly, mistakes I made that day, if not that hour, things I have not had any time to accomplish. Focusing on those things is easy. Focusing on my positive attributes is much harder. Some of us were taught not to brag. Some of us were taught the evils of pride. But for most of us, that ended up hurting our psyches.

Now write down three more words: How does *God* describe you? Think about it. We believe God *knows* each one of us by name.

We are "holy and dearly loved" by God (Col 3:12). God loves us so much that we are called the "children of God". (1 John 3:1). Those are two of the words God would use to describe you: *beloved, child*.

Many times, we feel oppressed by our lives. We may actually feel like slaves. Jesus promises, "You are no longer slaves . . . I have called you friends." That's a word Jesus would use to describe you: *friend*.

God also promises to dwell in us: "Do you not know that you are God's temple and God's Spirit dwells in you?" (1 Cor 6:19). You may not think of this as a word God would use to describe you, but it's true: God would call you *home*.

Beloved. Child. Friend. Home. These are beautiful words, and they are the ones God would use to describe you. It might be very helpful for you to spend a few moments reflecting on those words. Let them sink in. God *promises* to name you in this way.

The work we do, the care we provide, those are *part* of who we are, but those things cannot define us. We may be physically strong, which makes us a terrific caregiver for someone in a wheelchair. We may be able to live on very few hours of sleep, which makes us a wonderful companion for an Alzheimer's patient who wanders in the night. We may have a deeper well of patience than anyone we know, which is necessary to care for the children in our home. These are wonderful traits. But they are not the only traits you possess.

You may be a deep thinker. You may be a creative cook. You may be nimble. Good with your hands. Able to remember lots of jokes. A storyteller. Good with names and faces. You may love music or the ocean or finding a great bargain. You see how virtually none of these attributes can be boiled down to a job title.

In many cultures, particularly Indigenous ones like those of the Aboriginal people in Australia, or Native American populations in North America, people do not give "one-word" answers. They tell a story. These cultures understand there is always more to be understood about a situation when we understand the context, the setting, the spirit of the people, their emotional life.

The same is true of you. You are not defined by one aspect of your life. You are defined by many aspects of your life. Why not spend the next few days writing down beautiful aspects of you. Imagine our loving God thinking about you, delighting in you. What words would God use to describe you? God loves God's children. God will not speak ill of you. God loves you. How might God think of you? Could you think of yourself in that same way?

Back to Mary and Martha. Those dear women. Martha probably thought Jesus loved her because she made his favorite meals and kept a clean house. What if she had put down the work long enough to ask Jesus what he liked about her? Imagine what he would have said. Imagine what he would say about you? I suspect Mary knew exactly what Jesus saw in her. She knew "the better way" because she was in relationship with Jesus and with herself.

The same is possible for you. You can find your way back to the real you. You can find yourself buried under all this stress and care. You can find the person God loves. You were there all along.

CHAPTER FIVE

Isolation

Now Jesus was teaching in one of the synagogues on the Sabbath. And just then there appeared a woman with a spirit that had crippled her for eighteen years. She was bent over and quite unable to stand up straight. When Jesus saw her he called her over and said, "Woman, you are set free from your ailment." When he laid his hands on her, immediately she stood up straight and began praising God.

—Luke 13:10–13

At first glance, this is a story of physical healing. We have a woman with an ailment, and Jesus straightens her bent spine. But notice the words: she has a "spirit that had crippled her." One interpretation may suggest an evil spirit afflicted her body. But I think this story is about someone with a deep spiritual wound: depression, shame, guilt, exhaustion. The physical, and perhaps the spiritual ailments, had broken her. It had also isolated her from her community. She is bent over. People cannot make eye contact with her. They do not speak to her. They do not touch her. The opening sentence gives us more information about her than we might initially read. *Just then there appeared a woman with a spirit that crippled her* . . . She appears out of nowhere. No one noticed her coming and going. She draws no attention to herself, so no one realizes when she came in. She just appears.

While the story does not say so, I suspect this woman was in the temple all the time but was virtually invisible. The only reason she gets mentioned here is because *Jesus notices her.* She may have disappeared into the background to most folks, but Jesus knows there's a unique, hurting person in front of him.

As I write this, I begin to think about special needs patients. They draw attention when they are in public. There is the wheelchair, or the loud voice, or the unfamiliar facial features that tell everyone they are "not normal." I was in a library when a large group of adults with Down syndrome arrived. I could tell you where each one of them was seated (or not seated, as the case may be). They drew attention, not intentionally, but just by living life the way they know how. Even looking up things on the internet was a noisy affair.

I could tell you where the clients with Down syndrome were. I could not tell you where their caregivers were. Perhaps there were not enough of them. Perhaps they just did not warrant any attention. This is my point: the caregiver is often invisible. The world pays attention to the client, but not those who care for them.

The caregivers in the library were paid professionals. At the end of their shift, they could go home, leaving their charges to someone else. Caregivers who live permanently with their patients, such as a spouse or a child, do not have that luxury. We are talking about spouses caring for spouses with Alzheimer's disease or cancer. Parents with special needs children. Adults caring for their aging parents. When we are caring for family members with special needs, we can become all-consumed. The need is great, and our sense of responsibility is huge. In fact, we often disappear under the burden of the responsibility.

That burden weighs on us. We shuffle through our days, certainly unable to stand up straight and tall and face the world. And as our burdens continue without letup, we bend down more and more. We get depressed, and then we have no energy to lift our own spirits. We are lonely because of the spiritual depletion. And then we isolate, saying we don't have time for friends, and "who would want to be around me anyway?"

Look back to the ailing woman in the story. *She is bent over and quite unable to stand up straight.* I relate to her in deeper ways than I thought imaginable.

I attended a workshop several years ago on biblical storytelling. The storyteller takes a story from Scripture and "tells" it, using the exact text from the Bible, memorized, and told in their own voice. This is a way to take classic stories and have them come alive, not with new language or new interpretations, just with honest telling of stories that many of us have heard over and over again. The first story told in the class was this one of the bent-over woman. Our teacher was a young, handsome man with a goatee and dark eyes. He stood in front of us and said, "And just then there appeared a woman with a spirit that had crippled her for eighteen years. She was bent over and quite unable to stand up straight." He transformed into this wounded woman, bending low, walking slowly, moving to a corner of the room, trying to remain anonymous.

He continued, "When Jesus saw her, he called her over and said, 'Woman, you are set free from your ailment.'" Now he personified Jesus, standing with confidence, noticing the woman, walking to her. And then the storyteller bent over, as Jesus, so he could be eye-to-eye with "the woman" who was now just an empty space next to him. He bent over as deeply as he had as the women. He needed to be at the same level to heal her. He met her where she was. It was the simplest of gestures, but it was powerful.

We all need this: we all need someone who truly sees us. Someone who can bend to our level and hear a horrific story about the nightmare in our house *and just sit with us in our misery.*

When he laid his hands on her, immediately she stood up straight and began praising God. This is the moment of the miracle in the story. Jesus's healing touch makes her stand up straight. This is one of the few miracles in the Bible that does not suggest supernatural power. This is one story that shows the power of human touch. *Maybe* there was a physical ailment that needed correcting, but the story says it was her spirit. Jesus's touch restores her soul.

Jesus goes up to her and puts his hands on her. This could be the first human touch she has had in a very long time. Remember, no one looked at her; no one was talking to her. Her loneliness was back-bending. What made her stand up again? Human touch, human contact, human interest in her well-being.

We need human contact and human understanding. We need people who can relate to us. This is why support groups are critical. If you do not have enough time to meet with people once a week or once a month (and I beg you to make that time), find an online forum so you can read about other people who are as bent over as you are. It will make a world of difference.

We also need touch. Seek out affection from those who can give it to you in healthy, appropriate ways. Many worshipping communities have greetings, handshakes, or hugs, as invited, in their services. Some people acknowledge this is the only human touch they get in a week. You can also consider adopting a pet. Or exercise, even a little. The woman in this story had a spiritual ailment, truly. But she had also lost touch with her own body. Move your body. It will love you for it.

But while this woman had contact with another person, and it was transformative, she also had contact with the divine. This is an encounter with Jesus, whom Christians believe is God. When we are bent over, it is time to bring in a higher power.

In my Lutheran tradition, we profess that Jesus is equally human and divine. Many Christian traditions teach this. What is particularly mind-blowing about this perspective is we believe *God* came to earth and experienced everything humans experience. Jesus was hungry, thirsty, exhausted. He knew love and loss, laughter, misunderstanding, frustration. He understands suffering and even human death. Jesus understands spiritual suffering because he went through it. Read Matthew 24, the story of Jesus's agonizing night in the Garden of Gethsemane before his arrest and death. Jesus knows anguish.

When we pray, we are praying to God, who in the person of Jesus, bore a lot of emotional burdens. He cried. He got angry. He needed time away. He prayed. A lot.

I believe a person who prays *often* has a wide range of prayers. Yes, there are prayers of thanksgiving (see chapter 15 on gratitude) and joy. But there are also prayers of anger and frustration and questioning. God made us fully human. God expects our prayers to be fully human. Jesus brought his full emotional, human self to his prayer life, and you can too. Remember, Jesus met the bent-over woman where she was. He leaned over, meeting her in the emotional space where she dwelled. He did not lord his superiority over her. He came down to her level, a level he knew personally. No judgment, no empty cheerleading, no vague promises. Jesus leans down, touches her, and understands. He can do the same for you.

I've mentioned several ways to help you "stand up straight." This is not meant to disparage those whose bodies are not able to stand upright. Many people have suffered with the simplistic interpretation of Scripture that says broken bodies are not whole until they are fully functional. Simplistic understanding of these stories would make those with differently abled bodies wonder why God has not healed them. Pastor Zach Johnson, a pastor who lived with disability until his early death, taught me much about healing stories in the Bible. So did Pastor Cyndi Jones, a friend and pastor who uses a wheelchair. Healing comes in a variety of ways. While this healing story *does* have a physical healing, the spiritual healing is so much more significant.

No matter the state of your body, your spirit *can* be healed, and this is what Jesus understood. An important part of this healing is not written; after the woman had a spiritual healing, she was able to re-enter society. The people in the temple would have seen her face-to-face. Finally. She would be seen again. She would return to the community, fully present, fully recognized.

This is what we all need. Community. Friendships. Spiritual practices like prayer and devotional reading. Spending time with

Jesus. Support groups, either online or in person. Human contact is so critical. Spiritual contact is so critical. Depending on your personality, you will need a different combination of each. You need both. We all do. Make a change. Reach out. Re-engage your soul and your body. You may find the spiritual equivalent of "standing up straight." Your perspective may change. Your worldview may brighten. You may see solutions to problems that seemed insurmountable. No matter what, you will not be staring at the ground, you will be looking up.

CHAPTER SIX

Anger

The Passover of the Jews was near, and Jesus went up to Jerusalem. In the temple he found people selling cattle, sheep, and doves and the money changers seated at their tables. Making a whip of cords, he drove all of them out of the temple, with the sheep and the cattle. He also poured out the coins of the money changers and overturned their tables. He told those who were selling the doves, "Take these things out of here! Stop making my Father's house a marketplace!" His disciples remembered that it was written, "Zeal for your house will consume me."

—John 2:13–17

Years ago, I was at a Gay Pride parade in Los Angeles. As is typical there were protestors with delightful signs like "God hates fags" and "God created Adam and Eve, not Adam and Steve." I knew not to engage these beloved folks, but I could not help myself when I saw a sign that said, "God does not love you just the way you are." Having read a few chapters of this book, you know I strongly disagree with the statement. So, I did what any ill-advised young woman would do, I walked up to him and said, "Sir, I strongly disagree with what you are saying. God loves everyone."

The man was literally shaking with rage. He told me how wrong I was to think God could not hate people. Then he quoted the story above, how Jesus cleansed the temple, hating all the people inside. I do not remember much more about the incident (there was a television camera, I do remember that) but his red face, his shaking body, telling me how angry Jesus was, has stayed with me for almost fifteen years.

I did agree with one thing this guy said: I agree Jesus was angry. In my mind, Jesus was angry because Jesus cared, not because he hated. He did not want his Father's house, the temple, to be defiled. He was frustrated with the disrespect, and, I imagine, with how out of control the situation had become. It is hard to imagine this gentle teacher and healer making a whip of cords and driving people out, but the story is here, in several of the gospels, for a reason. "Righteous anger" seems to have gotten its start in this story. I also appreciate the last quote, "Zeal for my father's house will consume me." Jesus is certainly consumed. And "zeal" would be one word to describe his emotional state.

A lot of us get angry. A lot of us have very complicated feelings about this anger before it explodes, during and after. As mentioned in chapter 3, we might have a lot of guilt about feeling angry.

But anger tells us something about our situation. It can be our friend. Anger often tells us something unjust is happening. We might feel out of control or ignored. We might feel helpless or incredibly sad. Anger is a messenger. Rather than wanting to quelch it, ask anger what it is trying to tell you.

We must go beyond, "that person made me angry." It is critical to determine *what about that thing* made us angry. Were you made to feel stupid? Was there injustice? Were you frightened? Does the anger mask deep sorrow? What is really going on?

Anger has a purpose. Anger tells us something is wrong. And, used appropriately, anger pushes us to *do* something about it.

Anger is a messenger, and anger is an engine. It calls us to *move*. Could Jesus have cleansed the temple without getting really worked up first? It is hard to say. We cannot know his mind. But the gospel writers are very comfortable knowing his reaction was strong, and then he did something notable.

Most of us have been socialized against anger. "Don't be mad" is used as often as "Don't cry." Both phrases should be removed from the human vocabulary. Anger and grief are honest, unfiltered human reactions to real life experiences. Yes, we *should* teach our children not to hit each other in anger, not to destroy property, not to hurt themselves. But we need to teach our children how to experience, understand and express anger in healthy manners. Who am I kidding? We need to teach *ourselves*, adults, the same thing. Violence is *never* an appropriate way to express anger toward another living creature, be it people, children, or animals. Verbal abuse is never an appropriate way to express our anger. But this is a difficult thing to master, or, in some cases, even define. I had a family member who asked that I never raise my voice. It was considered an inappropriate expression of anger. I disagreed, but I wondered if this person had had traumatic experiences when someone they were close to raised their voice, and so I tried, not always successfully, to avoid raising my voice in anger. Our relationship deteriorated over the years, and I suspect part of the reason was because we were never fully communicating.

If we hold our anger in, our physical bodies suffer. We have all heard of the "fight, flight, or freeze" response, where all our systems go into overdrive when we feel stress. This is part of our design to stay alive when bad things threaten us. Heart pumps, blood moves, pupils dilate, breathing increases, adrenalin kicks in. If we needed to run from danger (flight), stay and defend ourselves (fight), or try to become invisible to prey (freeze), our bodies are preparing for it.

We certainly see this in animals and toddlers. If they have feelings, anxiety, or stress, or are reacting to threats after they are gone, animals and children move. Children have tantrums. Animals shake or stretch. All mammals run or climb or scratch. Our bodies have built up hormones and need to move them out. We know if we do not get rid of the hormones, they become toxic, making us sick, making us fat, making us lethargic. Our bodies need to do something with those chemicals and feeling angry is a sign that there is something within us that needs to be dealt with.

Our body reacts *appropriately* to threats with increased heart rate, adrenalin pumping, digestion slowing down, and muscles tensing. But if these physical reactions are not given appropriate release, our muscles ache, our head hurts, our blood pressure goes up. We can have digestive and sleep issues.

Many of us *feel* lousy a lot of the time. We assume it is lack of sleep or fatigue from all the caregiving. Sometimes we admit we have physical ailments due to stress. But what we do not realize is "stress" is anger reactions unreleased. You must express your anger appropriately or your anger could kill you. Literally.

Sadly, many of us were socialized away from anger in church. Christians do not get mad, we were told. "If you love God, you should not have negative feelings," is a destructive and popular message. And if you get angry, you need to repent. Honestly, this lack of emotional honesty has contributed mightily to the church losing its relevance in society.

In actuality, the Bible is filled with heroes who get angry. Jesus gets fed up with the moneychangers in the temple and responds with a whip. Samson may have had anger management issues, but he was also a servant of God. His rage was legendary, but God used it to defeat God's enemies. Of course, God also gets angry. There are *lots* of passages where prophets tell of God's fury, as well as God's desire to bring us back after God calms down. If we are made in God's image, we will get angry. It is part of our very nature.

So how can our anger be used for good, rather than destruction?

Many women are surprised to discover the "Mama Bear" within when their children are threatened. Mama Bear (or Papa Bear, let us not be sexist) is resourceful, strong, quick to act, has her priorities straight. She also knows how to use her anger instinctively to take care of her brood. "Don't mess with my kids!" is a wonderful phrase to hear as a child. Mama Bear is never going to say, "You know, I shouldn't get so worked up about things." She is just going to do her job and protect those who need her. Anger gives Mama Bear clarity.

The same may be true of caregivers or advocates or those defending the defenseless. We can get clarity on what matters and be motivated to do something about it. If we get in touch with our anger, we may be able to determine The Thing That Really Matters to us. Anger tells the truth. If we get in touch with that anger, we understand what drives us. You may be able to figure out what things need to change. Anger can be an important gift.

The key to understanding your anger is finding a way to channel it in healthy ways. No one wants to live in a constant state of rage. We need to control how we communicate when we are angry. We might need a physical release, we might need to journal or sing or talk to someone who can bear it, but we must not take out our anger on others or ourselves.

You know who can handle your rage? God. I have screamed at God, and found generally God says, "Yeah, I know, sit with me for a while." I have yet to hear God tell me to wash my mouth out with soap and call back when I can talk like a lady.

You may not have a lot of experience dealing with anger. You may only know how to stuff your feelings or explode. You will need some practice. If you are having a hard time managing your behaviors while emotional, talk to a professional or a trusted friend. The important thing to do is figure out why you are angry. Get specific. What injustices are you facing? Are you misunderstood? Are you discounted? These are all legitimate things to be angry about. Are you profoundly sad or scared out of your mind? That is going to bring up real feelings as well. See if you can figure out what makes you so angry.

After you know what you are railing against, you have options. Do you fight the injustice? Do you take flight from the injustice? Or are you stuck or frozen in this dilemma? Remember, these are the responses your body is hardwired to do—fight, flight, or freeze.

Sometimes the things that make you angry are inside you. You can work on your inner life to quell the anger. You can heal old wounds. You can confront those who have contributed to those wounds. You can seek therapy or visit a clergy person. You can surround yourself with love and support. You can battle the demons inside, or you can work to figure out how to release them. You can wonder if you are called to just freeze. Be still. Listen.

And sometimes the things that make you angry are external. You can change doctors. You can confront the office manager at the clinic. You can plan to have someone *else* call the insurance company, even once. You can work to change systems or legislature or policy. I will be honest, as I write this list, I hear a multitude screaming, "Yeah, RIGHT!" And that frustration with insurmountable red tape and limited choices is generally the thing fueling our anger. Can we fight it, or do we need to take flight from it? Do we need to freeze and pay attention to our own soul?

What do we do when none of these seem to be an option? I would first ask you to look very, very hard to see if there is another option. I am reminded of Native American wisdom, in which a tribe must look for twelve different answers to their question before deciding how they will proceed. I cannot think of twelve answers to my questions, but I can see how forcing that many answers *may* open something we had not considered.

Make a genuine list of ways you can live differently, even if most of them are nonsensical or impractical. You may also get a moment of levity, if you come up with solutions that include toilet papering a hospital administrator's office or painting yourself blue. But your anger has driven you to consider new options. Options are powerful. Options are action. And finding these options, making these moves, are all gifts anger can bring you. Sit with your anger for a while. Anger is your friend. What does anger want to tell you?

CHAPTER SEVEN

Knowledge

It is not the critic who counts: not the man who points out how the strong man stumbles or where the doer of deeds could have done better. The credit belongs to the man who is actually **in the arena**, whose face is marred by dust and sweat and blood, who strives valiantly, who errs and comes up short again and again, because there is no effort without error or shortcoming, but who knows the great enthusiasms, the great devotions, who spends himself in a worthy cause; who, at the best, knows, in the end, the triumph of high achievement, and who, at the worst, if he fails, at least he fails while daring greatly, so that his place shall never be with those cold and timid souls who knew neither victory nor defeat.

—Theodore Roosevelt

I had a happy childhood. I understand that is an incredible privilege. I had a good time as a young adult. I was able to go to college, I was able to pursue the career I wanted. I even had success in a very competitive workplace. Things went well. I was not deeply engaged in civil rights or health care or the legal system or racial issues. No one in my family was an alcoholic or profoundly mentally ill. We did not have violence in my family. Life was pretty easy. I was blissfully ignorant to the troubles of life.

Then life changed, as it always does. I got divorced. Family members died. I went bankrupt. We adopted a teenager. Now I know things.

And you know what? Some days I truly resent the knowledge I have. I hate that I know what it feels like to bury friends or to end a marriage. I hate that I know what my father looks like when he cries. I hate that I know what it feels like to stop loving and I know what it feels like to never stop hurting.

I know a few things about the horrible, horrible things people do to children. I know a few things about how completely inept people are allowed to work in jobs where there should be no room for error.

You may know how quickly the ambulance arrives when you call 911. Or what the flashing lights of a police car look like reflected against your house. You may know what a person looks like as they have a heart attack or a panic attack or a psychic break. You may know how terrifying a bad drug reaction is. You may know the side effects of certain medications or what a mess a bullet makes of a human body or how furious you can get when you are on the phone with an insurance company. These are things you would probably prefer not to know.

There is so much weight to this knowledge. There is so much pain. But there is something else: there is so much power. Because you know things, you have power over them. Yes, life is notorious for throwing us curve balls. But now you may actually know how to hit a curve ball. I do not mean to sound coy. But there is something really comforting about knowing you have already experienced some of life's most traumatic events. You have learned from them. It is wretched, accursed learning, but you have learned.

This is not meant as some Pollyanna explanation for *why* things happen. I am not trying to point out the silver lining in a storm cloud that is ruining your life. I am not presenting the good that came from a bad situation. I refuse to say, "All things work for good." But

I will argue that you *have knowledge, and therefore you have power.*
You've been in the arena, as Teddy Roosevelt put it. You know things
other people do not have a clue about. You also know something
about yourself and how you deal with very bad situations. Again, I
understand you would give back all the knowledge and power to *not*
know these things, but this is the situation in which you find yourself.

Make a list of the things you know now. Include the things you
wish you did not know. The list earlier in this chapter might be
helpful: Do you know things about law enforcement? or the Department of Child Protective Services? or rehab? Do you have perfect
knowledge of when your loved one is coming off a manic high? Do
you have a clear understanding of which people are safe and which
cannot be trusted? Can you set your calendar to when the bingeing
or raging or depression will come?

Are there benefits to knowing some of these things? Go ahead
and allow yourself some gallows humor if you must. Now consider
yourself an expert. There must be some difficult situations where
someone with your knowledge would be helpful. Wouldn't you want
someone like you around? Someone who would know what to do in
a crisis or conflict?

I remember speaking with a visitor after a church service. He was
telling me about trouble he was having with the law, and, as a person
without transportation, he needed to make sure he was on the bus
in time to get to the courthouse by eight thirty the next morning.

"Oh, dude," I said empathetically, "You miss that eight-thirty
deadline, you are screwed. Those bailiffs are not messing around."
You know why I could say that? Because a member of my family had
missed that eight-thirty deadline for a court hearing, and it was not
pretty. I did not need to say anything more to this new friend, but
he knew I understood him in a specific way. No judgment, plenty
of joining.

I have also had the experience of telling a foster parent that our
son was fifteen when we took him into our home.

"Oh wow," the foster parent says.

"Yeah," I say. And we both know that we both know the truth behind that simple exchange.

Think about the friends you would call when you are in crisis. You would call the ones who know something about what you are going through. I tend to call the people who understand mental illness or addiction firsthand when I need support. I call Person X when I need to talk about addiction, Person Y when I need to process unjust systems, Person Z when I need to vent about interpersonal entanglements. You may have a similar list.

You are now that kind of resource person. Again, you might gladly give up that status to remain ignorant. But life did not work out that way. You have knowledge that might actually be a gift for someone.

In some ways, we now know how strong we are. But we also know how vulnerable we are. We know life takes surprising turns. We know the best laid plans are folly. We acknowledge there are things we will never know. This is the most painful knowledge, the knowledge of limitation. The knowledge of disappointment and disillusion. Wow, do I hate knowing about disappointment. I was perfectly happy being clueless about disappointment. I loved not having a good grasp on loss. Sometimes the loss of my own naivete drives me to despair. Cruel people tell me it was about time I grew up. Compassionate people generally look at me with a certain level of pity and offer a glass of water.

Ignorance was bliss. But we were not put on this planet to remain ignorant. We were put on this planet to continue to evolve and grow. With evolution comes new experience, and with new experience comes knowledge. Hard-earned, not always desired knowledge.

Just as a child must learn the stove is hot by burning her hand, we have learned important life lessons that will keep us safer, stronger, healthier. There is pain, but there is also information.

An image comes to mind of an old warrior. Battle-scarred, weary. Still alive. Victorious. Lucky. Skilled. The warrior has seen things no human should see. The warrior may have done things no human should do. But that warrior is wise. He knows his limitations; he knows his abilities. He knows his enemies and his allies. He knows the way military operations work. He understands landscapes and weather and how to use weapons and tools. He can hide and run and fight. Hopefully he has had time for the war wounds to heal. He has had time to soothe old bitterness. He has come to accept all that life has dealt him.

He is to be admired. I draw near to him. I want to hear what he has to say. Perhaps the warrior chose this life. Perhaps he was thrust into situations he never would have desired. But he is here now. And he knows things.

Whether or not we chose it, we know things. We are warriors. We are also teachers. You might share your knowledge; you might just let it shape you. You join the millions of others on this earth who have learned, the hard way, the truths of this life. You have joined the ranks of the wise. And no one can take that away from you.

CHAPTER EIGHT

Time

And Joshua spoke to the Lord and he said in the sight of Israel,
"Sun, stand still at Gibeon, and Moon, in the Valley of Aijalon."
And the sun stood still, and the moon stopped, until the nation
took vengeance on their enemies. . . . The sun stopped in mid-
heaven and did not hurry to set for about a whole day. There
has been no day like it before or since . . .

—Joshua 10:12–14

This is an obscure story in the Hebrew Bible, in which the Israelites,
led by their heroic leader Joshua, have been on the battlefield for
hours. God has promised Israel the victory. Joshua, the dynamic
young commander of the army, prays for God to stop the sun so he
can have more time to defeat his enemies. He has assessed his situation and knows he cannot get the job done in the hours remaining.
He prays for the sun to stand still, and it does.

When I scan my to-do list, I wish there were more hours in the
day. It would be *amazing* if we could just stop the clocks and have
more time between when the kids leave for school and when they
come back. What if we could have six extra hours in a day to clean the
house or run errands or catch up on deadlines? I long for this miracle
in my own life. I would *love* to have the sun stay in the sky longer. I
would even promise to use that time for good, efficient things, and
not to binge another season of my favorite television show.

But let's be honest: more time might be great, but there is something wonderful about the sun setting and the world going to sleep. For as many times as I wish there were more hours in the day, just as often I drag myself to bed with just one prayer, "Thank God this day is over. Thank you for rest."

Time is a strange and fleeting thing. It is a precious commodity. It is a resource. It can be wasted, it can be saved, it can be spent. It can be planned for. Time can be changed, lost, squandered, used up in the blink of an eye. As John Lennon so famously said, "Life is what happens while you are making other plans." How many times do we make a plan, thoroughly research it, parse out each participant's role, worry about it, talk about it ad nauseum, only to have the entire enterprise chucked at the last minute? Someone gets sick, one of the kids throws a tantrum, traffic gets balled up and the carefully crafted timeline falls apart. It is enough to drive anyone to utter despair.

It is bad enough when an appointment or vacation goes awry. What about our entire life? There are only so many sunsets left. This is a sobering realization. We do have a limited amount of time on this earth. Some people realize life is short and start to live more freely. They take more vacations, they relax a bit more, they savor conversations and meals and beauty. Others react by trying to pack the most efficiency possible into each minute. They cram their schedules. They make mile-long "bucket lists," that is, the list of things they must get done before they "kick the bucket." They want to live as much of life as they can.

Tell me, which one of these strategies makes the most sense? The one in which we realize we have a limited amount of time, so we start to enjoy life and do less, or the one in which we pack as much as we can into those limited hours? Some of us will pick one option, some will pick the other. Perhaps you can take a few moments now to think about which one you would choose. If you had but a week to live, would you rush to see as many of your friends and family as possible? Or would you do the opposite, filling your last days with new adventures *away* from the people with whom you spend so much time with now? If you only had a few days or hours left, how would you spend your time? The answer tells you a lot about what you care about.

You do not need to apologize for the plans that immediately came to mind. There is no *right* answer to the question of what you would do with only a week to live. But perhaps you can start living that way *now* instead of hoping you will get some insight into when that last week will be.

Time, like money and love, must be held lightly. Whenever we hold onto our money or our love too tightly, life becomes painful, or at least, life becomes small. When we decide we cannot spend any extra money or love, we start to become stingy with those things.

The same is true about time. When we are stingy with time, our experiences are limited. Of course, when we become too generous with time (just like money and love) we run the risk of being depleted. Where is the balance?

I would recommend experimentation. Try doing a little less. Try doing a little more. See which one feels better for you. I must confess I am constantly readjusting the amount of time I give over to volunteer work, family, rest, exercise, socializing. I feel the very best when I have a good balance of each thing. Of course, there are weeks when I socialize more than usual, and my volunteer hours suffer, or I give more time to freelance work, and my family life suffers. Again, it is a balancing act, and that simply has to be okay.

One of my coaches recently asked me, "What are your 'non-negotiables?'" What were things I insisted on doing every day to keep my balance? I listed several things I like to do a lot, things that ground me and make me happier. But none of them were nonnegotiable. Any one of these loving, important things could be dropped if another demand or "something better" came along. I realized this was a problem. If there are ways to spend my time that make my life better and contribute to my overall well-being, I need to make them a priority. I will likely be saying this to myself for the next twenty years, but perhaps I am getting closer to making these schedule decisions.

And here is the challenge. Time is a resource, like any other of our resources. We can and should value and respect those resources, but if we obsess about keeping them or losing them, life becomes unnecessarily conflicted. How can we bring grace to ourselves as we manage our calendar?

I return to the story at the beginning of this chapter. Joshua, a great man of God and warrior, prays for the sun to stand still. That is a miracle. Sure, miracles still happen, but the likelihood of one of us being able to pray and make the day twenty-eight hours long (or forty or ninety, should we become truly desperate) is low. I mean, think what it would do to our DVRs. Or the timer on my coffee maker. No, this is simply cannot be done.

So, I've gone for a different option. I often *pray for the day to seem longer.* That is, I have often prayed for God to help me make the most of the hours I do have. I pray for focus, for lack of distraction, for meetings to run efficiently and for factors that ruin timelines to be held at bay. Is that a miracle? What do you think? Does prayer work?

I believe it does. But I will remind you I believe prayer changes *our* hearts and minds as much as God's mind might be changed. Every mindfulness practice, like meditation or prayer, will teach that those moments of silence or intentionality *do* help our brains function better. Our blood pressure goes down. We become more flexible mentally and emotionally. Our neuro-connectivity in the brain improves. Doesn't it make sense that as we pray (or meditate or sit in silence for centering) we prepare *ourselves* for a better day? The Dalai Lama meditates one hour every day. If the day is particularly busy, he meditates for two hours. It is so counterintuitive, to take more time in spiritual practice when we are busy. But apparently the Dalai Lama knows what he is talking about.

Prayer does help us prioritize what is best for us. As we pray about our schedules and the things we care about, prayer helps us realize what truly matters. Clarity may come.

Patience may come.

Acceptance may come.

Compassion may come.

All these things will help us manage our time more wisely. And hopefully the mindfulness will give us acceptance when our schedule gets disrupted.

I recently taught a workshop on creativity. I asked the assembled crowd of busy people what kept them from being creative. There were the usual answers: fear, shame, not enough talent. Finally, someone said, "I just don't have enough time."

"Not enough time" seems to be the excuse for just about every good idea. People cannot get sober because they do not have enough time. They cannot get out of debt. Cannot exercise. Cannot go to therapy. Cannot volunteer. Cannot. Cannot. Cannot.

This is true until it is not true. No one has enough time to do anything, if that is what they tell themselves. There is not enough time to do the laundry, clean the house, feed the kids, sleep. We can convince ourselves there is not enough time in the day to eat or sleep, right? Basic needs get taken away for. . . what?

Keep a log of how you spend your days. Mark down all of it. Errands, driving, watching TV, sleeping. Caring for others. Doctor's appointments. Preparing meals. Eating. There are lots of nifty apps for time tracking. Now, are there places where adjustments make sense? As I write this, I think of some fallow hours I have every night. I spend those hours with a little reading, maybe a little disengaged television watching. I am tired at the end of the day. That is OK. I work a lot. Should I sleep differently, and have more energy during waking hours? Should I put an exercise bike next to the television so I can use that time more effectively? Am I becoming a control freak? I find when I try to schedule too tightly, I shut down. I also find having no structure makes life hard. What works for you? Or perhaps a better question: Is the way you manage time working now? Or, could you try something different?

Another gift you can give yourself is the understanding of what constitutes an emergency. Do you need to make a decision or act right now? Yes, the bleeding child needs to be cared for. Yes, the dog needs to be caught before it runs into the street. Yes, some medical decisions need to be made immediately.

But other decisions *do not* need to be made immediately. As new foster parents, figuring out what was urgent and what was not was a *lifesaver*. We get such a sense of urgency in our caregiving, that we lose sense of what is an emergency and what can wait. I loved the book *The Martian* by Andy Weir. Astronaut Mark Watney is stranded on Mars and must figure out how to survive. Written in the first person, Mark explains how he thinks through the decisions he needs to make. Frequently he decides what solutions need to be found immediately, and which ones can be figured out later. This organized thinking, crisis management versus long-term solutions, saves his life multiple times. I constantly admired his ability to know which crises were urgent and which crises could be faced another day. Caregivers do well to understand which things are urgent, and which are not.

Here is another evil little truth about time. We are truly not in control of it. And we need to be honest: sometimes that is the part about time we hate the most. Here I have spent several pages encouraging you to take charge of your calendar, to make decisions, to analyze your use of time, but sometimes, it just gets away from us. Doctor's offices are going to run on their own schedules. The traffic slows down in front of you. Your mother shows up twenty minutes early. "The best laid plans of mice and men often go awry," Robbie Burns wrote, embarrassing men and rodents throughout eternity.

Let me throw one more curve ball in this discussion about time. Jesus offered us eternal life. Most Christians imagine that means we will spend eternity in heaven, or paradise, or nirvana, or whatever elevated state you might imagine. But we are living in eternal life *now*. Everyone who came before us, everyone who comes after us, we are all part of a river of time that has been flowing since God first hovered over the "formless void" pre-creation. I find comfort in that. I matter to God, which is already amazing. I matter to God who knew everything since the beginning of the world and will know everything into eternity. I am not just a blip, and neither are you.

At the same time, we are part of a vast, eternal universe, and the fact we did not get the laundry folded before we went to bed does not really matter in the grand scheme of things. This "crisis" is real to us but is just a blip on the radar of eternity. I remember reading my teenage diaries, with all these stories of being furious with my mother, "this is the worst thing that has ever happened," etc. Now, decades later, I honestly cannot remember ever being angry with my mother. Of course, I was. It is written in indelible ink in my fifteen-year-old self's diary! Today it does not matter. At the time, it was the Biggest Deal Ever.

There are many, many things in our lives that will not matter in the long run. Time management is one of those things. Relationships will always matter. Our schedules will not be what matters. As the saying goes, no one on their death bed says, "I wish I spent more time at work."

God is an eternal God. You are part of the eternal story. You can afford that ten minutes to do nothing. Or do something wonderful. You are living forever.

CHAPTER NINE

Wrestling

So Jacob was left alone, and a man wrestled with him until daybreak. When the man saw he could not overpower him, he touched the socket of Jacob's hip so that his hip was wrenched as he wrestled with the man. Then the man said, "Let me go, for it is daybreak." But Jacob replied, "I will not let you go unless you bless me."

—Genesis 32:24–26

In this famous story, Jacob, a rascal and cheat, wrestles all night with God, or an angel of God. As the story goes, Jacob is marred for life by the encounter, walking with a limp from that day forward. Interestingly, God does not overpower Jacob while they are wrestling. This is an amazing statement. God does not defeat Jacob in the wrestling, but Jacob is changed.

How do we wrestle with God? The most accepted practice is in prayer. Some of us consider prayer to be a sweet, maybe even saccharine experience. Some of us know prayer as an intimate, sweaty, fervent experience.

Sometimes prayer is very formal. The person offering the prayer or meditation feels like they are entering a sacred space. They clear their mind. They may close their eyes and fold their hands. They may kneel on a rug, or always sit in the same chair or cushion. Sometimes people use lofty language. For those of us who were raised in a tradition that used the King James Version of the Bible, we may even use Old English pronouns like "thee" and "thine" in our prayer.

Other people enjoy a much more informal style of prayer, preferring to think about prayer as "just talking to God." This takes away some of the distance people feel about a Heavenly Father, floating somewhere far away from us. I remember so clearly visiting a teenager in a local hospital when I was a chaplain. I sat with her for a few minutes, and she asked if I would pray for her, because she did not know how. I agreed, and quietly prayed a very simple, very honest prayer about her situation and her concerns. After the "Amen," she looked at me sort of incredulously and said, "Well, I could have done *that*." She made me laugh, but I was pleased. She *could* do that. Anyone can talk to God. But many of us are afraid to express our true feelings to God. We think it is a sin to complain or scream or tell God how horrible the situation is. We believe we are only to be grateful, to bow humbly, to enter God's presence with respect. Is it possible we had parents who told us we could never backtalk, and we have assumed the same stance with God? We think we need to find the good in every situation, and then let God know we have found the blessing.

The Bible gives us plenty of examples to prove otherwise. People *wrestled* with God, and not just literally, as in the story of Jacob. People of great faith often have prayers of deep doubt and despair. They do not apologize for these feelings. They simply express them as honestly as possible. This level of trust in God is a worthwhile goal. Think about your human relationships. Most of us describe our true friend as "the one I can say anything to. I can just be myself." Why don't we expect the same acceptance from God who created us and loves us?

The psalms are filled with examples of people pouring their hearts out to God. Psalm 142 says, "I pour out my complaint before God, I tell my trouble before him. When my spirit is faint, you know my way." Lamentations 3:55 proclaims, "I called on your name, Lord, from the depth of the pit." You see the psalmist practically shaking his fist at God, lamenting, crying out, "Help me! You promised!" And of course, one of Jesus's most famous prayers was when he quoted Psalm 22 from the cross, "My God, my God, why have you forsaken me?"

Generally, though, when a psalm starts with this intense lament, there is an acknowledgment of God's presence in the second half of the psalm. The writer *knows* God is listening and will care for them. They have learned they can name their fears and frustrations because God continues to abide with them, no matter how badly they feel. This relationship with God becomes much more intimate, and in that intimacy, more gratitude, more obedience, more transformation occurs in the lives of those who pray so honestly.

Some prayers cannot be put into words. I was praying with a friend during a healing service in my congregation. This friend came toward me, grieving the imminent death of her partner from a very fast-moving cancer. She was devastated. She knelt and took my hands in hers. We immediately burst into tears. I leaned my face next to her ear and whispered, "God, it's too much," and we both just cried. It was the best prayer I ever prayed.

I will never forget hearing a young man scream during congregational prayers in an otherwise peaceful setting. "God!" he yelled. And then he let out a howl. God knew exactly what the man was trying to say. Romans 8:26 promises when we do not know what to say in prayer, the Holy Spirit intercedes on our behalf "with sighs too deep for words."

Still others believe prayer should not be about output. Meditation and mindfulness flip the script: we do not express, we take in what the spirit wants to give us. We breathe in cleansing, we still our minds and listen. Meditative practices allow for this listening, rather than telling. This practice is not for everyone and is called practice because it is not easily mastered. When our words stop and silence comes, the Spirit (or Wisdom, or Love, or Beauty) has all the space to enter into us, wordless. It is simply an experience, sometimes fleeting, sometimes only recognized much later.

Different souls crave different connections. I spent years feeling guilty that I did not pray enough during the day. I'm not sure what "enough" prayer would be, but I sensed I was falling short. It was not until I realized I was filled much more significantly with meditation, both silent and walking, that I discovered a much more satisfying prayer life. I also gave myself a break about prayers when I realized I talk to God throughout the day, asking for guidance, letting God know how I feel about things, wondering about God's will and presence in my life. Instead of having one big phone call at the end of the day, I am more of a "text as you go" kind of praying person. This works for me, because my relationship with God is much more constant, much more integrated into all aspects of my life. It works for me. It may not be right for you.

Others may also find activities like walking to be prayerful. Rev. Dr. Monica Coleman writes about baking and biking as two repetitive movements that are healing and important in her spiritual life. Martin Luther encouraged digging in the ground to reconnect to God if prayer and Scripture reading were not enough. Many of us find exercise or repetitive movement, like knitting, to be important spiritual connections. God is good, and knew we needed many ways to connect with God.

Below is perhaps the most famous prayer in the Christian world. Jesus's disciples asked him to teach them to pray, and he replied using words we now speak in the Lord's Prayer,

> Our Father who art in heaven,
> Hallowed be thy name
> Thy kingdom come
> Thy will be done
> On earth as it is in heaven.
> Give us this day our daily bread.
> And forgive us our trespasses,
> As we forgive those who trespass against us.
> Lead us not into temptation
> And deliver us from evil.
> For thine is the kingdom and the power and the glory,
> Forever and ever.
> Amen.

When I was a chaplain in a hospital, we were encouraged to offer this prayer for people. At first, I balked against it. I thought each pastoral call needed a specific prayer, tailored brilliantly by me, the Pastor of the Moment. I could swoop in, assess the situation, and pray the perfect prayer. But then I came to realize how important tradition is. When people are frightened or stressed, the familiar is a wonderful thing. To hear "Our Father who art in heaven" was, to these patients and their families, sort of like hearing the strains of a familiar song. They were transported to another place, or, as I described earlier, they were taken immediately to a sacred space.

The Lord's Prayer may lose its effectiveness in our lives when we pray it by rote. Try considering this prayer from your role as caregiver:

Our Father who art in heaven, hallowed be thy name

Many of us struggle with the word "father" because we cannot help but think of the man who gave us birth. For some, this word brings extremely warm, safe memories of a loving provider. For others, this word brings extremely painful, cold, cruel memories of abuse or neglect. Many modern translations have changed this opening phrase to "Mother/Father" or "Parenting God" or "Abba." While this may help those who are injured, there are others who find that language even more distracting.

In any case, this opening phrase was used by Jesus to tell us the God to whom we pray wishes to be in loving relationship with you. God wishes to be "Papa" or "Daddy." Someone you would like to call several times a day just to check in, who will be happy to hear your voice. To "hallow God's name" means to show reverence. We start this prayer by saying how much we love and honor God. God made us and the world in which we live. God is the God of *all* of us: of our broken family members, of our ailing bodies and minds, of all the people who work in the broken systems of healthcare and courts and education and social security. God is even the God of your insurance providers' customer service department.

Thy kingdom come, thy will be done
On earth as it is in heaven

Again, this part of the prayer shows our trust of God. We want God's will to be done on earth. We profess God's will is already being done in heaven. We often think of God's kingdom as some perfect place with no war, no suffering, no pain. We like to think anger and hatred would be outlawed in God's kingdom.

And yet, over and over again, Jesus told his disciples, "The kingdom of God is at hand." This is not something that is coming in the future. God's kingdom is already here. We are living in it *now*. How can that be? How can we say God's kingdom is here when we see so much that is wrong with the world? Clearly God's kingdom is *not* a place of perfection. But it *is* a place of God's presence. God's spirit moves freely among us. Perhaps *that* is what is needed to maintain God's kingdom on earth: God's spirit moving in our lives.

This phrase is also pivotal in the lives of beleaguered caregivers because it reminds us God's will needs to come, so our will needs to subside. If most of us truly thought about what we are asking here, we'd choke on the words. We want our will, every day, in every way, to be done. I constantly think of how much happier I would be if everyone just did things my way and saw things my way. That would be fantastic. And yet, early on in this classic prayer, Jesus tells us we must give up that control. It is a miserable suggestion. And, apparently, crucial. Healing. Foundational.

For the rest of this chapter, I would like to introduce you to a version of the Lord's Prayer you may not know about. It comes from *The New Zealand Book of Common Prayer*, published by the Anglican Church in 1989.

With the bread we need for today, feed us.
In the hurts we absorb from one another, forgive us.
In times of temptation and test, strengthen us.
From trials too great to endure, spare us.
From the grip of all that is evil, free us.

For you reign in the glory of the power that is love, now and
forever. Amen.

I find this prayer to be especially helpful because our needs are
named first, and then the request follows. It is a more honest repre-
sentation of the struggles we face in our family lives. It also claims a
promise that however we wrestle, whatever needs we throw at God,
God has a loving response. Our most basic needs are met through
our providing God.

I first meditated upon this prayer during the early months of life
with our foster son. Every meal was challenging. He hated most foods
we put in front of him and was only able to articulate his displeasure
in myriad, unpleasant ways. Whenever we came upon a food he *did*
like, he ate it voraciously. We had to lock food cabinets. We fought
about food constantly. We consulted doctors who gave us physical,
psychological, and emotional reasons for his eating problems. "It's
trauma!" "It's attachment!" "It's a control issue!" "All foster children
go through this!" "Be flexible!" "Be more structured!" "Don't force
him to eat!" "Let him eat everything he wants!"

This was our world. And then I come upon this version of the
Lord's Prayer which simply asks

With the bread we need for today, feed us.

God knows what our son needs, even when we do not. God knows
why food is so complicated for our son, even when we do not. God
knows what nourishment each of us needs, beyond food, beyond
drink. God knows our hungers. Reflect upon your hunger and what
you "need for today." Ask God to feed that hunger.

In the hurts we absorb from one another, forgive us.

If ever there was a prayer for hurting families, this is it. I am
grateful for this perspective on sin, that *we absorb* the pain of those
around us, either as victims or enablers or simply observers of the

bad behaviors. We absorb those hurts, and those hurts affect how we live. There are cycles of sin and evil, and each of us is susceptible to those cycles.

Family systems theory explains how every member of a family (or other small or large organization) is affected by every other member. Emotional responses, traditions, worldviews are all shared by the system. One family member does something, it affects everyone. Children affect parents, grandparents affect children, we absorb each other's hurts and love. It is truly beautiful and terrifying in equal measure. This prayer acknowledges this, saying, Forgive us, God, when the ripple effect becomes a tsunami. Stop those cycles. We place our trust in You.

In times of temptation and test, strengthen us.

Parents raising children are certainly always feeling "tests." The kids want to find your limits. They want to know they are safe, and so they are constantly testing to find out if they can count on you or not. It is exhausting. I would pray this prayer often as a parent.

But what about the temptations listed here? Temptations to lash out or punish? Temptations to "give you something to cry about?" These are dark, ugly temptations. But for some of us, they are real things we wonder about. This prayer is especially important for those who are experiencing the temptations of the overwhelmed.

Another set of temptations for caregivers are unhealthy means of escape: alcohol, drugs, pornography, gambling, unsafe sex, abusive relationships, overeating. When we are exhausted, we reach for *anything* to help us feel better, or, more accurately, to numb the pain. These temptations pose real threats for caregivers, especially for caregivers who feel isolated, misunderstood, or underappreciated. This prayer is for those terrible times of temptation.

The first step of prayer is to admit there is something to pray about. We come with a certain level of trust that God can hear our problems. I believe God then gives us the courage to be honest with ourselves and others. Instead of hating ourselves for the temptations we are experiencing, can we love ourselves into acknowledging the pain we are feeling? Which leads us to the next petition:

From trials too great to endure, spare us.

"That which does not kill us makes us stronger." Frederick Nietzsche wrote it, and the beleaguered have been quoting it ever since. This phrase seems slightly more acceptable than "Every cloud has a silver lining." But when you are in the middle of crisis, not seeing *any* relief in sight, it is hard to believe either of these platitudes. Are there trials that are, in fact, too great to endure? Yes! People die of illness or injury. Marriages end. Despair causes people to commit suicide quickly or slowly. Please, God, spare us from those trials that are too great to endure . . . There are things that are bigger than we can manage on our own. Spiritual, emotional, and physical exhaustion comes when we try to do it all ourselves. Help us God. Help.

From the grip of all that is evil, free us.

Modern thought and reason have tried to dismiss evil as a term used by the superstitious or ignorant. We try to explain away evil behavior with psychoanalysis or sociological processes. But most of us know what it is to be held in the grip of evil. We see despair, violence, misunderstanding, cruelty. There is a lot wrong in the world. Does it matter where it comes from? The important thing is to acknowledge it exists, and we need God's help to combat it.

I know a night minister, a person who cares for people on the street, frequently working from sundown to sunrise. One night the minister was out in his usual get-up, a clerical collar and jeans. He was waving to people he recognized as he walked down the street, greeting them by name. An old man, probably on meth, called out to him.

"Hey pastor!"

"Hey, how are you?" The night minister did not recognize him but wanted to show kindness.

79

"I'm all right. Have a good night!" said the man. The pastor moved on. After a moment, he heard the man call out again.

"Hey, pastor, do you see the demons around me? Will you pray for me?"

The night minister turned quickly on his heel, coming up to the man. "Yes, right now!"

And he prayed for the power of God to protect this man from the demons that surrounded him.

Had the pastor seen actual demons surrounding this child of God? No. Had the man seen demons? Yes. They were very real to him. And he knew he could ask the pastor for prayer and support and comfort. No questions asked. It would not have been helpful to say, "Oh, there's nothing there. You're fine." The man was tormented by evil of some kind and needed prayer.

Your experience of demons may not be nearly as extreme. But we can agree that there are things that are bigger than we can defeat, and we need God to protect us.

The Lord's Prayer in *The New Zealand Book of Common Prayer* ends with:

> For you reign in the glory of the power that is love, now and forever.

We love because God loves us. We have the power to continue living in our families because God loves us. In my mind, God's power is completely based in God's love.

Several images come to mind as I write this. They are of big muscular men holding tiny newborn babies. Strong, powerful fathers who are capable of tenderness and love. The firefighter's huge hand holding the tiny foot of his little daughter. A bodybuilder's gentle kiss on the forehead of his sleeping child. Yes, the father is strong. But he is also loving. And that is where his power lies.

I also think of the mama bear image: the female who can defend her child against intruders, but then returns to the den to feed her children. The babies are comforted by her presence as well as the knowledge she can protect them.

Which leads us back to this image of wrestling with God. If a young child is angry with that powerful father, and punched him with all his might, the father may wish to correct the child's violence, but (a) the punch would not hurt the father and (b) the father would want to know what was going on with the child. I do not wish to infantilize us—we are God's children, but we are not juveniles. Still, many of us are afraid to wrestle with God because we think God cannot handle it, that God will send us away. It is not in God's nature.

Prayer is an opportunity to connect with God's love and God's power. It is a chance to tell God what is really going on in your life, to share honestly your concerns and feelings. Just like a human relationship, your relationship with God deepens when you share of yourself most completely. And because you have been so honest, you will be more available to receive the blessings and comfort and instruction God wishes to give you.

If you have not had a good relationship with God, perhaps it is because you have not been able to connect to the God you were told about. God was always some Old White Guy in the Sky with a long beard and lightning bolts coming out of his hands. Has God always been some invisible force? Who wants to connect to either of those images? There are a few ways to cultivate connection to God. One is to think of a time when you did feel connected to God. You may have to reflect on this for a while, as it may have happened in a setting you would not have expected. You may realize you felt closest to the Divine (or Light, or Beauty, or Peace) when you first saw a newborn. During a sumptuous meal. Hiking the Grand Canyon. In a morgue. Some of us feel it in worship spaces, but many do not. Consider what gave you that sense of connection and see if you can recreate that wherever you are now. Meditate on that experience and see if it can be brought back.

If that does not work, perhaps you can reflect on a characteristic of God you admire. Safety. Kindness. Creativity. Focus on that characteristic, thank God for it, marvel in it, ask God to apply it to your current situation. See if that brings you closer to God.

Sometimes God moves quickly, and you feel connected rather quickly. Sometimes God moves slowly, and the connection is not immediate. I choose to believe God knows what God is doing, and your connections will come in a customized way which God knows is best for you. You may find yourself arguing with God as you are waiting for the right revelation. Hey, now you are arguing with God! You are a modern-day psalmist!

This is how you come to a more honest relationship with God. It may be uncomfortable to be this vulnerable. You may have been taught to only come to God with praise, that God is too busy to hear your little problems. And that prayer life has not worked for you. Try being vulnerable and see how it goes.

Tell your side of the story. But then listen as God tells God's side of the story. God's story has wisdom and strength and power and revelation to be found. And those seem like things we could all use.

CHAPTER TEN

Meaning

Curly: Do you know what the secret of life is?
      [holds up one finger]
Curly: This.
Mitch: Your finger?
Curly: One thing. Just one thing. You stick to that and the
      rest don't mean s**t.
Mitch: But, what is the "one thing?"
Curly: [smiles] That's what you have to find out.

—*City Slickers*,
Castle Rock Entertainment, 1991

I may be arrogant enough to think I can write a book, but I am not arrogant enough to think I can tell you the meaning of life. But movies can do it. *City Slickers*, a movie produced by Castle Rock in the 1990s, provides a few answers to life's hardest question: Why are we here?

The exchange above took place between Curly, a tough cowboy played by Academy Award winner Jack Palance, and Mitch Robbins, the unhappy guy next door played by Billy Crystal. If you remember, the movie starts with Mitch and his friends realizing they are in major life crises: failed marriage, inappropriate relationships, general malaise in work and personal life. Mitch's friends surprise him with a two-week trip to drive cattle in the Southwest. Mitch says he cannot go because he promised his wife a trip to see relatives. But his wife sees the existential funk he is in and encourages him to go. Hilarity ensues, along with the life lesson taught by the head of the cattle drive, Curly. Curly is intimidating, playing with knives, and telling Mitch, "I crap bigger than you." But Curly also understands the meaning of life. And perhaps more importantly, Curly understands that each person has their own unique definition of what that meaning is. I will not spoil the movie, it is worth looking at again, but Mitch figures it out. Of course, he does. It's a movie.

I was a young evangelical Christian. The strength of the evangelical movement is the 24/7 commitment to Jesus Christ. All of our lives were shaped by our understanding that Jesus died for our sins, and our job was to live our lives in service to Christ. So before middle school, I was already asking what the meaning of life was. Perhaps I should not blame this on my Christian upbringing. Perhaps I am just precocious. But universally, in my evangelical circles, the answer to my question, "Why are we here?" was, "To love and serve God."

The good news is we understood all people could serve God. You did not need to be a minister (girls couldn't, anyway) to serve God. Homemakers were serving God (this was a refrain that needed to be sung a lot in the 1970s), teachers, farmers (lots of them in my community), were all serving God.

For a hot minute, I thought if our sole purpose was to love and serve God, why did God need us? Wasn't God all powerful? Is it weird to create a world, just to create servants? Or, more disturbed, is it weird to create people just so people could love God? What kind of issues does God have?

I moved past that position, more or less, later in life. But the question remains, why are we here? Ironically, I still come up with the same answer, to love and serve God. But not because God has issues, because God wants relationship.

One Jewish rabbi explained it to me as *tsimtsum*, a Hebrew concept of a place where God isn't. (There are other chapters in this book that would claim there is *no place* where God isn't, but bear with me.) This teaching says when God created the world, God filled every space. In order for God to create, God needed to withdraw a bit, so there would be a finite space where other creatures could exist. This withdrawal allowed the cosmos to be created, in a place where we might have some free will and go about our business. And our business, in God's plan, was to be in relationship with God. Sure, God gave us a rich life and experience and wants us to enjoy all of it responsibly, but God also wanted relationship.

Now it makes sense that we were created to be in relationship with God. Well, what about the gazillions of people who do not have a relationship with God? Depends on where you sit, but some of us believe those people are *still* in relationship with God, they just do not know it. That might be enough to make your head explode if you are an evangelical, or, if you are an atheist, might make you angry because your free will is being tampered with. I don't make the rules, I just write about them.

But maybe you are one of those people who was taught their purpose was to love God. And you know, like any of us with an honest heart does, that we fall short, like every fifteen minutes. We find comfort in knowing God wants us to love people and animals and the planet, and so maybe we can love God by loving others. Actually, God encourages such things. Good! Now we only have to love others. Other people? Oh dear. Again, we fail that, maybe every two hours. Oh, is this just me? Anyway . . .

The truth is, humans need purpose. Humans need a reason to live. Each of us has our own "one thing," to quote the illustrious Curly from *City Slickers*. What is your "one thing?"

A helpful way to determine this is to write a mission statement. A lot of organizations do this, when they feel adrift. They ask themselves, "Why does this organization exist? Why are we here?" And they drill down on core values, which helps them remember why their founder started this thing in the first place. Spoiler alert: No mission statement is "To make as much money as we can as quickly as we can." You may be surprised to learn this. But all organizations had a purpose when they were founded, even if it was to be the best widget maker this side of the Mississippi.

So, what matters most to you? Other chapters in this book will help you determine that. I think of a couple who was trying to figure out who would fly to be with a dying mother, who would take the kids to their graduation, who would clean the house, who would check in on the neighbor. It was too much. So, they had to decide what mattered most. What was their mission statement? You might also consider this as a list of priorities. And guess what? You cannot have eight priorities. You probably can have three, and that's only if you are also drinking protein shakes and sleep eight hours a night.

This couple decided someone being with Mom while she passed was the number one priority. They talked to their kids, and to their surprise, the kids agreed. So, one parent went to be with Mom, no matter how long that would take. Another went to graduation. The house remained a disaster zone for two months. Their priorities were lived out. It was a terrible time, but they lived with integrity.

When we find our meaning, our purpose, we tend to live with more integrity. Decisions are made based on our values. Unimportant things fall away. You may actually discover more focus and more freedom.

Mihaly Csikszentmihalyi calls this "flow," a mental and spiritual state where you are so intensely involved in the One Thing that you are focused, productive, and rarely aware of how much time you have spent. Csikszentmihaly says "flow" is possible for everyone, from rice paddy digger to fine artist. We find the thing we were created to do, and the work flows out of us. While we do not always get the luxury of having our "flow" also be our life's work, we all can get to "flow." Csikszentmihaly talks about this as a very positive, energizing state of being.

It might be hard for you to imagine: a positive, energizing state. I believe this comes from living out your values. What matters most to you? Justice? Peace? A calm home? Making sure the people around you are safe and well fed? Cleanliness at the cost of sleep? Does your own sense of well-being get a vote? Does your marriage take priority over speaking at a city council meeting? Maybe, maybe not. But you get to decide how your values influence these decisions. I know a man who discerns which job he should take based on what it will teach him about himself. I used to think that was a self-centered, narrow way to choose a job. Now I see his wisdom. He is open to what life will teach him, and he values what he learns about himself. What are you learning about yourself? Could self-knowledge be the "one thing?"

That feels self-centered I know, but I am wondering if truly knowing oneself is actually another way to love and serve God. God made us. God had an idea of who you could be, and God has been luring you toward that idea ever since. God never promised an easy life, but God did promise love. God loves people and things God values. You have value. What was God's dream for you? It may not be to be a professional opera singer, even if you are a really good singer. It may not be to be mayor of your town, even if you were elected Most Likely to Succeed. Maybe God gave you deep wisdom, or compassion, or strength. Maybe God made you a mighty thinker, or a prayer warrior. What is that one thing? I know this runs counter to the previous chapter that discussed how you are not defined by one thing. But we are talking about an essence, which may not be named with one word. We are talking about your being, your soul. Oh yeah, remember that thing? We were focusing on that in this book.

Soul care includes knowing and loving that soul. And most of us have lost the time and connection with our soul to truly know it. Perhaps that is the one thing. Finding your soul, buried under the to-do list and the vast ocean of feelings. That essence of you. That essence knows your purpose. Spend some time there, and see what wisdom emerges.

CHAPTER ELEVEN

Pause

When the entire nation had finished crossing over the Jordan, the Lord said to Joshua, "Select twelve men from the people, one from each tribe, and command them, 'Take twelve stones from here out of the middle of the Jordan, from the place where the priests' feet stood, carry them over with you, and lay them down in the place where you camp tonight.'" Then Joshua summoned the twelve men whom he had appointed from the Israelites, one from each tribe. Joshua said to them, "Pass on before the ark of the Lord your God into the middle of the Jordan, and each of you take up a stone on his shoulder, according to the number of the tribes of the Israelites, so that this may be a sign among you. When your children ask in time to come, 'What do those stones mean to you?' then you shall tell them that the waters of the Jordan were cut off in front of the ark of the covenant of the Lord. When it crossed over the Jordan, the waters of the Jordan were cut off. So these stones shall be to the Israelites a memorial forever."

—Joshua 4:1–7

I heard a story on NPR this morning about how social media is harming our bodies. We have all heard the warnings about mental health and "doomscrolling," the practice of rapidly moving through a social media feed and stopping to read outrageous or tragic posts. This story was suggesting our bodies hold all that trauma, and it is harming us, especially young people. The antidote for social media overload was to lie quietly in a darkened room with no sound for forty-five minutes a day. I understand the thinking; it seems many people do not even shut off screens before going to bed, scrolling or watching videos until their eyes close. But the idea of forty-five minutes in silent darkness seems luxurious and, to be honest, literally impossible for most people.

But hitting the pause button on our life, stopping the input, changing up the scenery, stepping off the hamster wheel of life feels very, very right. We all know we are supposed to do it, but it is a struggle to unplug, shut down, get outside, and drink a glass of water.

God called us to Sabbath. I think God knew we would not naturally do it for ourselves, so God told us to do it *for God*. Honor God with a Sabbath, is the commandment, when in reality, God knew we would also be honoring ourselves.

"Great," you may say, "now I feel guilty for not taking a break. This is *not* helpful."

Okay, let me offer you a different way to consider taking a break. Let us think about rituals instead. Rituals bring order to our lives. They make meaning. They also allow us to pause from the day-to-day and move into something special. They mark time, they celebrate milestones, they bring us into sacred spaces.

When most people think of the word "ritual" they think of religious ceremony. Weddings, funerals, some sort of symbolic gesture with extra meaning attached. All participants are supposed to know what the ritual means because we were either taught specifically or we were raised doing it and took it in through osmosis.

Rituals are not always fancy. Think about wedding receptions or birthday parties. How many times have you told yourself (or your impatient spouse or your overtired child) "We can leave as soon as they cut the cake." Do we wait for the cake because we are all dying for dessert? Maybe. But we also know the cake cutting is the last important ritual of the event. Actually, at a wedding reception, "tossing the garter" might be the last important ritual of the event, but many of us avoid that ritual because (1) we are married and our spouse tends to get annoyed when we pretend we are not or (2) we are tired of displaying the fact that we are *not* married to a roomful of people.

Sporting events are full of ritual, from singing the national anthem, to cheering for our team, to questioning officials' calls, or to the amount of food we eat while we are there. You might call it "habit" or simply "being a fan," but really, it is all based on rituals.

Rituals are regular, reliable events we participate in. We know how to behave because of rituals. We love ritual. Ritual is a framework onto which we hang our life experiences. We sort our lives through ritual. We make sense of things through ritual. Ritual helps us define time and space and ourselves.

Think about ritual in your family. For most of us, the first things we consider are holiday celebrations. My family has a Christmas ritual in which we all sit around the tree and wait patiently while the youngest opens the first gift, then the next oldest, then the next, then the next. Once everyone has opened a gift, the youngest opens another. We go on for at least an hour like this. It may have felt fun and festive, but there was a need to pause, to notice, to spend time appreciating every single gift and the recipient of that gift.

Another ritual, maybe a tradition, in my family is "the note." If you received a small, lightweight package under the tree, it may be cause for great celebration. "The note" would be a handwritten note, usually written by my mother, but later written by me or my brother, frequently in funny and clunky rhyme, describing a gift that was too large to wrap. To this day, if one of us opens a gift with a piece of paper in it, we shout, "It's a note!" and know something wonderful is about to happen. Again, a pause. The author had to stop and write the poem. The reader has to stop and read. There is anticipation and joy. A moment in time.

I was well into my adult years before I realized how carefully my mother had to plan out Christmases to make sure we all had the same number of gifts. This was another very sacred ritual in our family. One year my brother got a drum set for Christmas, a huge, expensive gift. I was getting three or four nice but not extravagant gifts. So, my mom wrapped two or three really tiny, cheap presents for my brother, just so he would have the same number as me. He could barely hide his incredulousness at socks, a book, a puzzle, while I was opening everything I had asked for. At the end of the night the doorbell rang, (no note this time!) and my brother went to answer the door. A friend of my parents had set up the entire drum set on the front porch. When Tim opened the door, our friend played a great rim shot and my brother literally fell over. The smaller gifts were truly unremarkable, but there were four, just like there were for me. Giving and receiving an equal number of gifts, opened one at a time, is a sacred family ritual for me. When I married into a family that opened gifts helter-skelter with no rhyme or reason, I was pretty sure universal order had been destroyed.

So, yes, family celebrations tend to be a great place for ritual. But we do ourselves a disservice if we do not give more of our regular, reliable day-to-day occurrences their proper due.

Who makes the coffee in the morning? Do we sit together to drink it? Do we help with dressing or bathing? Do we eat certain things on certain days? Who attends sporting events? Who does not?

These shared experiences, these shared agreements, are sacred. They are holy moments where two or more people connect. If those rituals are broken because of illness or separation, they are to be mourned. They have been shaping your life in significant ways and now they have been altered. Do not dismiss the little things. How many widows will say the early evening is their loneliest time? If they looked back on those hours they shared with their husbands, they may have been unremarkable. A simple dinner. A quiet night at home. She may have been disappointed that he read the paper or played with the dog instead of talking to her. But now he is gone. Their rituals are lost. It was a chance to pause at the end of the day and just be.

It may be helpful to think of several rituals you currently have and honor them. You might be thinking, "Eesh, all we do is sit around watching television every night!" But this activity frames your lives together. If one of you was missing from that activity, the ritual would be broken. Everyone involved would notice the change. These rituals are to be honored.

My son and I tended to have arguments in the car every morning on the way to school. This is not remarkable. Many families would report this activity. One morning we were on our way and about three blocks from our house he started an argument. We bickered back and forth for a few minutes. I made the same turn right I made every day, just before the park.

"We always argue on that street," he said, pointing behind us.

I laughed. I realized he was right.

"And you always laugh right here." I scanned my memory. I had not really thought about the exchanges we had every time we were driving to school. But he was right. We always argued on the street, we always stopped before we got to the park. It was a ritual. And my son sensed it long before I did. He named it long before I would have been able to.

I was so touched by that moment. He was noticing patterns, even when I was not. I am the adult. Aren't I supposed to be the observant one?

This is an important thing to consider. As caregivers, we may be too busy or too distracted to notice patterns. The one receiving our care is probably keenly aware of the patterns and they come to depend upon them, or dread them, as the case may be. I suggest these rituals are to be honored. Perhaps they can be held as sacred in your life.

We are constantly told as caregivers that our children long for consistency. The quicker you can put a baby on a schedule, the better. Your child, no matter what age, longs to know where the boundaries are. The same is true for other patients. Your Alzheimer's patient functions much better when they operate under a routine. Instead of thinking of these structures as oppressive or depleting, try thinking of them as beautiful rituals.

You may have a person in your life who exhausts you with their rigidity. Vegetables may not touch meat on a plate. Towels must be hung in an exact manner. All tags must be removed from clothing. I am pretty laid back and do not understand these requests, but I try to remember these rituals are important for the other person. They are telling me what they need to get through this moment. For any number of reasons, they need things to be just so. Is it trauma-based? Maybe. Is it an obsessive-compulsive disorder? Maybe. Is it a need to have a little bit of control in a world that is nothing but chaos? Sure. When we are barraged by demands, if only we can hear the words and ignore the tone (good luck with that, by the way), we can discern information on how hard life is for this person. Or at least how important this bit of ritual is for them. We all need ritual. Some of us just need it in more places than others.

I am writing these words for myself as much as I write them for others. Having to create so much routine is exhausting. Thinking of these routines as sacred rituals may help. It may not. But if we can think of more of our activities as life-giving, rather than soul-sucking, perhaps we can feel better. If we can approach these rituals as a high priest approaches the holy of holies, knowing that we enter sacred space each time we create one of these rituals, perhaps we can find wonder in it all. Certainly, we can find beauty.

We have talked a lot about finding beauty in the tiniest of places. A relatively calm meal. The first time someone says thank you when we do something "right." (This *almost* erases the memory of the four thousand times we were yelled at for being "wrong," but we take what we can get.) A glimpse of connection in the middle of a chaotic evening. The moment when you and your mother sigh and relax simultaneously. These are beautiful, sacred, holy moments. They may be a random gift; they may be the result of ritual. We have created a safe environment. We have removed some of the anxiety around not knowing what to expect. We have paused. We know how to behave here: we behave this way every time we do it. Bath time, walks, meals, tucking in at night. Can you think of these mundane experiences as sacred? You are carving out a pause, a ritual. You are acknowledging the little moments that create a lifetime. This matters, to them, and to you. Be blessed.

CHAPTER TWELVE

Gratitude

Piglet noticed that even though he had a Very Small Heart, it could hold a rather large amount of Gratitude.
—A.A. Milne, *Winnie the Pooh*

Some people grumble that roses have thorns; I am grateful that thorns have roses.
—Alphonse Karr

The nursing supervisors at County Hospital realized they needed to help their staff deal with anxiety, depression, and burnout. They decided a monthly "rap session" would be a good idea. There would be a meeting after all three shifts on the first Friday of the month. The break room was brightened with a big bouquet of flowers, a variety of baked goods and a coffee cart. The nurses would have a chance to "let their hair down" and talk about their patients, gossip about doctors, and let off some steam. The first few meetings were nice enough, but everyone left feeling about the same.

The supervisors came up with a plan. "Let's have everyone tell their most recent high point and their most recent low point." Each nurse told the stories of their best moment, and then their lowest moment. The highs were pretty high; it was fun to hear everyone's stories. But the lows were really low. After the meeting, everyone felt a little worse.

"Maybe we shouldn't talk about the bad stuff," someone suggested.

"No, we need to be able to talk about it," another nurse said. "I'll scream if I have to hear about how great everything is when in reality *it isn't.*"

Others nodded their heads. To ignore the pain would make it worse. Then someone suggested they change the order of events. Tell the horror stories, certainly, but *end* the meeting with joyful stories. And that is what they did. Everyone was given a chance to tell the worst thing that had happened to them since their last meeting. And then everyone was given a chance to tell the best thing that had happened to them. People reported feeling better after the meetings.

Then the rules changed again. Everyone was given a chance to tell the worst thing that happened to them. But if you wanted to pass, you could. You were not forced to remember a negative experience. But *everyone had to tell a blessing.* Everyone *had* to give an example of something good that had happened. At first people were resistant to having to come up with an example. But then the idea caught on. People looked forward to the meetings. They began taking notes during the month about the positive things they wanted to share. They knew they could always come up with something bad; it was the good things they wanted to remember.

Now the last things the nurses heard before they left their meeting were stories of warmth, humor, success, love. Their brains held on to those memories and the nurses' spirits were lifted, hours, even days later. They were seeing the roses beyond the thorns.

Our brains hold on to the most recent things we experience, positive or negative. Why do you think dessert is served last? How many movies have you loved until the lousy ending? It is why dates end with a kiss, meetings end with a handshake, why bedtime rituals are so important. The last word *matters.*

Many spiritual practices include evening prayer or meditation. Studies have found these practices are substantially more fulfilling if they include prayers of thanksgiving. One of our most lasting spiritual practices was created by Ignatius of Loyola in the sixteenth century. St. Ignatius was a priest and theologian in Spain. He formed the Society of Jesus, also known as the Jesuits. He created several spiritual practices that included meditation, prayer, and various mental exercises. One of his most famous practices is called the Examen, or Ignatian Examen.

The Examen requires a person to end each day by recalling events and encounters and determining where they could have done better in their relationships to God and others. They also consider where they most deeply felt the presence of God. I would suggest this practice can be very useful in seeing where God is present. Enter this practice with curiosity and wonder; where is God, even in the painful times. The challenge would be to find God, rather than focus on one's own failures and successes.

Another examen is one of gratitude, where you think back on the best thing that happened, or the most beautiful, or the most gracious, even if it is a tiny moment of joy in the middle of a miserable time. (This may vaguely remind you of the maddening search for beauty in chapter 2). You focus on that one moment of grace and thank God for it. As Meister Eckhart said, "If the only prayer you said in your life was 'thank you' that would suffice."

It is not surprising that people who are grateful tend to be people who are happier. I know a bishop who answers the question, "How are you?" with a confident "Grateful," and I am sure she is having a better time than me. Her answer does not mean she is always happy; her answer means she insists on being grateful.

Several studies asked one group of people to journal three things they were grateful for during the week. Another group was asked to write down three times they were hassled or annoyed during their week. Unsurprisingly, the people who kept gratitude journals reported being 25 percent happier than the hassled group. Interestingly, they *also* reported fewer health complaints and exercised an average of one and a half hours more per week than the unhappy group. They also slept better.

Another study had people write down one thing they were grateful for *every day*. Those people soon reported they had become more compassionate. They were able to offer more emotional support for others in need. How can this be? Believe me: if there is a way to strengthen my ability to be supportive, I'll take it. Now.

If we fill our brains with gratitude and connectivity to the world, animals, people, and nature around us, of course we will begin to empathize with that world. We may finally see things more clearly, people more clearly. We are busy appreciating our external world, and therefore our hearts are opened to it. Piglet was on to something.

There is an iconic concept about computers and computer programming: garbage in, garbage out (GIGO). It means if you input lousy data or program code, the computer can only spit out lousy data or program code. We realize the same is true with people. If you expose your brain to garbage all day, the brain is only capable of spitting back out garbage. A child who only watches sports all day will not suddenly be able to quote poetry. Of course, this goes beyond children: all people's exposure to violence, pornography, rough language, and so on deeply affects their ability to relate to the world in positive, healthy ways. We are starting to realize social media is bad for our mental health. What we let into our brains affects our wellbeing.

This is not just about a bad hobby, this is about forming a bad habit. Our brains *love* order and similarity. Once we start on a certain path of thinking, our brains want to keep thinking those thoughts. Neurons are firing, pathways are being created in the brain that move in a certain direction, making the same connection over and over again. Our brain rewards familiarity, our brain *expects* certain things to remain the same. We seek out negative information, we start to crave negative information. New information has to circumvent pathways we already have in place. It *can* happen. But it can be difficult.

Brain science time:

Mood regulation is managed by our brains, in conjunction with our blood sugar and other chemicals in our body. The hypothalamus an area of the brain, about the size of an almond, found just above the brain stem. The hypothalamus releases a groovy enzyme called dopamine. It's sort of like a "reward" neurotransmitter. It's like when your puppy gets a ginger snap after doing the trick you are teaching him. When dopamine is released by the hypothalamus, we feel good, and our brain makes the connection. "Do that again!" the brain says, as it wants to continue to feel that good. This is part of the reason why people get addicted to food or drink or exercise or sex. It feels good, the brain releases dopamine and we long to get that feeling back.

The National Institute of Health ran a study in 2009 that found that the hypothalamus sends out a bunch of dopamine when people express gratitude. People were thankful for something in their life, and boom, they began to have a sense of well-being. Their brains liked what they felt. They wanted to continue to feel good, so people continued to be grateful. The brain says, "Do that again!" and we seek out more things for which to be grateful. It is an attitude adjustment. Instead of looking for negative things, and continuing in that pattern, we are now constantly on the lookout for more things to be grateful about.

Remember, you are *changing the pathways in your brain.* This takes a little time. Start a gratitude journal or try the gratefulness examen every night and see how it goes. If you have a terrible day, you may have to work to find a moment of gratitude.

There is an old joke about a farmer who consistently buys his boots one size too small. He would come into the Tack and Feed store once a year and buy a new pair, wincing as he tugged size 10 boots onto his size 11 feet. After several years of this, the clerk finally asked him why he put himself through such torture.

"I get up before the sun every morning, eat my breakfast in the dark and listen to my wife snore. I stand in my field every day and watch the wind blow away my crops. My cow is sick, my horse is ornery, my wife hasn't said a kind word to me in fifteen years. After she burns my dinner and complains about our children who we never see, I get to sit down and pull off these boots. It's the only joy I can count on every single day."

I bet if he started a gratitude journal with an entry about his boots, in a few days, he may be able to find one other thing for which he is grateful. Perhaps it is the softness of his pillow. Or the satisfaction he gets from washing his coffee cup. It could expand from there. If the theories about gratitude and compassion are correct, once he noticed the good in his life, his heart would open a little. He might have some compassion for his beleaguered wife. He might find forgiveness. He might see some good in her as well.

You can see how gratitude can change the dynamics of your family. You may also be so miserable you cannot imagine being grateful for anything you experience. As a foster/adopt family, we were often in support groups where the leader would ask us to name something we liked about our kids. Many of us had kids with really difficult behaviors.

"Tell the group something you like about your kid," the leader would say.

There was usually this uncomfortable pause. It was sad. Parents could not come up with one thing they liked about their five-year-old. Or their teenager. Or the pile of kids in their house. As bad as it was for the parents, imagine how hard it was for the kids, living in a place where there was no joy.

In this setting, a little dark humor finally emerged.

"I have to say I really admire this kid," one father said. "He knows what he wants, and he demands it. He'll scream and scream and scream, like for hours."

Many parents nodded wearily.

"But damn that kid is tenacious. He won't stop. He stands up for himself. I admire it. I mean, I want to kill him, but I admire it."

Another family laughed. "Our kid got arrested last week, and you know what? We were grateful he didn't have a weapon on him. Maybe we should send him a card, 'Good job not using a gun in the commission of your crime.'" Fairly miserable thing to be grateful for, but there it was. Someone high-fived them.

"My kid reduced his temper tantrum after dinner last night. It was only twenty minutes," the mother turns to the dad. "Remember when it was two hours every night?" The dad laughed and lied: "No, no I do not remember that," and he started twitching to great comic effect.

"I honestly don't know how they do it," a parent said softly. "This life of theirs is impossible."

"Our life is impossible. But so far, it hasn't killed any of us," some-one else said.

Now the room felt fierce. Empowered. Committed. Today they were grateful for the chance to laugh. For the people with whom they could laugh. For the shared courage. Maybe they treated their kids a little differently after that meeting. Maybe the effects only lasted twenty minutes. But there was a little hope, a little camaraderie.

This was more than a 'feel-good' exercise. This was a rewiring of our brains. We started the conversation in a mindset of despair. We could not think of one good thing about our kids. Then we began to build on a new way to look at our kids. There was laughter, shared experience and ultimately, compassion.

Maybe you need to tell a dark joke about your situation. Where is the humor in the bed pan? In the dirty dishes? In the seemingly pointless series of tasks you have to do for your loved ones? It is hard to find the funny, but that might help.

Or find the smallest thing for which you are grateful. The taste of your coffee in the morning. The flower you saw coming up from the crack in the sidewalk. The friend you remembered today. Maybe you could write them a note, maybe they called you. Connection. A memory. A song. Your favorite sweatshirt. The kindness of a cross-ing guard, or an ER nurse. Or the insurance company manager who *finally* answered your questions after you were on hold for an hour. Find the thing. Notice it. And offer thanks.

It's good for you. It's good for your brain. That sounds like a win-win to me.

CHAPTER THIRTEEN

Hope

The young girl woke on Christmas morning,
Eager to see what was under the tree.
She had an unusually cruel father, who had warned her
She would find nothing good under the tree.
Ever hopeful, when she got to the tree, she discovered a large
pile of manure.
She ran to the shed, took out a shovel and started digging.
Her father thought she had lost her mind.
Undaunted, she exclaimed, "There must be a pony under
here!"

Two dreams come to mind. I dreamt the first one during a very dark period in my life. I was in a cinder block cell, buried underground. There were very small rectangular windows near the top of the cell. Those windows were just above the ground line. They let sunlight into my cell, but no one walking by would be able to see me inside without bending down and investigating closely. I was claustrophobic in that space and hopeless. I saw a pair of feet walk toward my window. I did not even have a voice to cry out, so deep was my despair. But the face of a friend of mine appeared in the window. "Hey, what are you doing in there?" She saw me, then she saved me.

In another dream, I am once again in a cell. In this dream, I know I can break out, but it will require a great deal of effort. The cell first lengthens and becomes very tall. I try breaking through the cinder blocks, no luck. I try to reach the tiny window to wriggle out, no luck. I dig through the dirt floor with a shovel. No luck. Then I use the shovel to whack at the cinder block wall until it finally crumbles, and I am free. But once I am out of my prison, I discover I am in the middle of a dusty wilderness. There are dirt hills around me, dirt pathways that lead to nowhere.

I am not defeated. I want to find people. I am sure there are people somewhere. I long for connection. I run long distances, looking for the sprawl of a city. There is nothing for miles, but I am not daunted. I keep looking. I rest for the night confident I will find companions as soon as I wake. At no time during this dream do I feel lonely or panicked. I am sure I will find people. I have hope.

When I woke from that dream, I cried. Not because of the isolation. I cried because I was *sure* I would find people, and, in fact, I did by the end of the dream. I found a town full of strangers who welcomed me vigorously. I *knew* it would end that way. And I *knew* the welcome would be warm and healing, even before I had received it.

This seems like the very definition of hope.

> Faith is the assurance of things hoped for, the conviction of things not seen. (Heb 11:1)

In this famous quotation from the book of Hebrews, faith, hope and conviction are all used in the same sentence. Imagine if you moved the words around:

> Hope is the assurance of things we are convinced of, the faith in things not seen.

> Conviction is the assurance of things we have faith in, hope for things not seen.

Hope may be the same as faith. It may be the same as conviction. Most of us would say that is not true. "Hope" is in the subjunctive; that is, we want something to be true, but there is no certainty. In English it is the difference between it *will* happen and it *might* happen. We *hope* it will happen: the subjunctive case.

The Spanish language is *full* of verbs in subjunctive case, and it speaks to the culture of Spanish speakers. We hope for many things. *Esperanza.* We have faith in many things. But we are also realistic: we know things do not always go the way we plan. *Ojala* ("if God grants it"), is a phrase used frequently in Spanish. We understand nothing is guaranteed, all is a gift. The chance for a gift is the hope; whether or not it arrives is reality. If life gives us a pile of manure, we dig: *Ojala*, there is a pony under there.

In my dream, I spent a lot of energy looking for people. But I was not dogged. I *knew* I would find them. And I acted accordingly. I kept going. In some ways, it is the difference between a person who *tries* to do something, and someone who just *does* it.

These dreams point to the thing I longed for: connection. In our darkest hour, we feel so alone. We feel imprisoned, trapped in solitary confinement. We lose hope when we cannot find connection to companions or saviors. In the spiritual practice of hope, we are looking for connection. *Who* or *what* we connect to may be the surprising element to hope.

National Public Radio ran an amazing story about Dr. Jim Olson, a pediatric cancer doctor and researcher. Dr. Olson has treated and cured thousands of children with cancer. He has also seen thousands of children die. He tells a surprising story of how he came to love this work. It was during his internship. He had just been with a family whose seven-year-old daughter had lost the battle against brain cancer. He grieved the loss of every child, and this death was very painful.

As he walked home that night, he was joyous, almost bouncy. "This was not how I usually was," he recalled. He wondered what made him so happy after such a bad day.

He sat for a long time thinking about his day. He kept returning to a conversation he had with the parents of the little girl. He expected them to be grieving, of course, but worried they would come at him with anger and blame. Instead, they rushed to him and hugged him. "Her death was as beautiful as her birth," they said, thanking him for his care and honesty throughout the ordeal. They were able to celebrate her short life, even on the day it ended. He realized he had been part of something truly remarkable, and it was energizing.

This family understood they would only have a brief time with their daughter. They realized there was no hope for recovery. A different type of hope came into their lives. They realized they could hope for deep human connection with their daughter until the very end. And they seemed to understand, even in the first hours after her death, that there would be an emotional and spiritual connection with their daughter forever. Hope was not lost.

It is so difficult to remain hopeful when we are caring for a person who will not recover. Many people have reflected that caring for an infant may be exhausting, but we have hope that they will become more and more self-sufficient. Caring for an elderly person is difficult because they become less and less self-sufficient. They will not be "getting better," even if certain symptoms improve with medication or rest or diet. Sometimes the only hope a family has in that situation is to hope for a "good death." I love what the parents said about their daughter's death being as beautiful as her birth. As my grandfather was nearing death, I remember saying to my mother, if we believe God has written the book of our life, God has written the last chapter as well. We can have hope that the last chapter will have beauty and grace and peace. We can certainly hope for connection, between the dying and the mourners, in that last moment.

Many of us who are giving care to the deteriorating become discouraged by the loss of relationship. Our spouse is now a silent shell. Our parents no longer recognize us. Communication lessens, deteriorates, and then disappears. How do we maintain the human relationship when our patient is slipping away?

I visited a patient who had suffered a terrible brain injury in a diving accident. In fact, doctors had just performed a test to determine if she was brain dead. The patient had no family visiting her. For all intents and purposes, her brain was no longer functioning. Was she still human?

I sat at her bedside and put my hand inside hers, not sure if she would even know I was there. After a moment, her hand squeezed mine. I tried not to overreact. I calmly said to the nurse, "Uh, she's squeezing my hand." The nurse was not phased. "Yes," she said. "The brain is short-circuiting. It's nonvoluntary. Like a reflex."

So, I am holding the hand of a woman who seems to be squeezing back. The medical professional tells me it's nonvoluntary. The patient does not mean to be making a connection. *But a connection is still being made.* I think of that moment *often.* Two people, holding hands, one may or may not be brain dead. But it was still two humans holding hands.

I invite all caregivers in the most lonely of circumstances to explore the connections that are still being made. Many of us believe in the moments after a person dies, their spirit lingers in the room. So even though the body is deceased, a spiritual connection can be made.

We may be sitting with a mute Alzheimer's patient, or a comatose accident victim, or an autistic child. There are no words. But could our souls still be mingling? Many of us have had experiences of making eye contact with someone who cannot speak, and there is a fleeting recognition, or a spark, or just the flick of interconnectivity. It cannot be denied. It must not be dismissed. Spiritual connection happens in the briefest of moments, and it is profound.

I sat at the bedside of a mute child, simply watching television with him. I kept my hand on the rail of his hospital bed. After about twenty minutes I felt his tiny pinkie finger move to be against mine. I did not make eye contact. I did not say another word. I just let that tiny connection hold. Did it make him feel better? I hope so. Did it warm my heart? Yes, it did. I would like to think the child could sense that warmth. He had been seeking it. I would like to think he felt it. Our spirits joined, even for a moment. That is what the human experience is all about.

Of course, we all worry about when the physical relationship will be ended by death or distance. That loss is real and cannot be avoided. But the spiritual connection can live on. I return to a phrase from that opening verse from Hebrews. What we are talking about is *the conviction of things not seen*. It is those unseen things, those unspoken moments, that spiritual connection that bring us hope. Language may not be adequate to describe it. But our souls respond, and that cannot be taken away from us.

Our son came into our lives when he was fifteen years old. He had been in the foster system for too many years. His case file was filled with stories of disappointment. Biological family members had betrayed him, the foster care system had failed him. Legal teams had missed the mark, mental health services had fallen short, the people who were entrusted to care for him on every level had proven inadequate over and over again. And yet, when he met us, he quickly determined we might provide him with a safe home. He interviewed us for hours while we played with him and other youths. He asked probing questions, he shared enough of himself to seem vulnerable. He was taking risks, trying to find a permanent home and adoptive parents. After he had lived with us for a few months, he asked what we liked about him.

"You have hope," was the first thing I said, really without thinking about it. Why, after all the heartbreak this boy had experienced, would he dare to believe he could have a better life? Why would he dare trust new people? Why would he imagine stability and comfort were possible, maybe even love? Because deep down, under all the layers of denial and anxiety and defensiveness, lived a soul who hoped for connection. It continues to be my absolute favorite thing about my son. Hope is overwhelming and powerful. Hope is based on our soul's need for connection, and a strong belief that somewhere out there is another soul who wishes to connect.

I return to the dream I described in my opening to this chapter. I ran and ran and searched and searched, knowing somewhere, there were people. I never lost hope. My longing for connection drove me forward. And I was satisfied. We all can be satisfied. Our souls can connect.

You are likely exhausted. You may be afraid you will never connect again. But there are *always* people to meet. There are *always* sunrises and flowers and delicious food to discover. There are *always* ways to know yourself more deeply. And because of this, there is reason for hope.

CHAPTER FOURTEEN

Forgiveness

To err is human, to forgive, divine.

I wish I was good at forgiving. In my mind, to forgive is a highly desirable virtue. It makes us the "bigger person." Pettiness has been eschewed. Magnanimity reigns supreme. And, as the proverb says, "to forgive is divine." To be good at forgiving is to become one step closer to divinity. That sounds like a worthwhile goal, especially if I have gotten a good night's sleep.

I have struggled with forgiveness all my life. I had something of a charmed early life, where people were rarely terrible to me. I did not have to learn to forgive trespasses. Talk about privilege! I do not have a lifetime of practice of forgiving. But it was only recently that I realized one of the key barriers I have against forgiveness.

I was talking to a therapist about a long-standing resentment I hold. This grudge has been gnawing at me for years. I was finally ready to face how disruptive it is in my life. I came to my therapist, ready to deal with it.

"I think I need to forgive," I confessed.

"Okay," my therapist said. "What do you want to forgive?"

There was a long silence, which is rare for me. Nothing came to mind. Bad feelings came up, but I could not name the harm. I could not come up with the tangible things this person had done to hurt me. Did I need to forgive them just for being insensitive? No, that was not strong enough. Did I need to forgive them for being clueless? Did I need to forgive them for being judgmental? That was closer to the truth, but that did not work either. My therapist gave me a few other prompts, but none of them rang true.

"This is why you are stuck," my therapist said.

I could not name what the offense was, therefore, I could not forgive the offense. After much thought and another two hundred therapy sessions, I have a few ideas about this. People are mean, people dismiss me, and people are self-centered. People hurt my feelings. And somehow, I still have a hard time describing what the matter is. There are several factors, one of which is that I think I deserve it. The people who hurt me the most are the ones who say something I agree with, at least on some level. Someone tells me I am insensitive, and I know I missed something about them, so "insensitive" might be accurate. (In reality, "human" and "not a mind reader" are probably more accurate.) When someone accuses me of not knowing what I am doing, I usually have a little voice inside me that says, "They are right you know! Your secret is out!"

I have a hard time forgiving a meanie when I think they are right. I am also really slow on the uptake. I have enough balls in the air at any given moment that it is hard to let in another thing, in this case, a cruel remark. I am slow to react sometimes, and only after I leave a difficult conversation do I realize how bad it was.

Another deep-seated issue in my life is I was raised in a brand of Christianity where selflessness is regarded as the highest virtue. To suffer, to turn the other cheek, to regard everyone else as more important than oneself was drilled into me as a child and beyond. I do not blame my parents: we were swimming in this water of selflessness as holiness, and the messages were everywhere. We are a sturdy lot; we take it on the chin and keep going. The fact that most of us do not have stomach problems or alcoholism is truly a miracle.

Because I do not truly name what hurts me, I do not have a lot of experience with forgiveness.

This may be your problem. You may be upset, but you have never really articulated what the matter is. You feel like a victim, or put-upon, or dismissed, and it sits in your body as depression or illness.

Or, possibly, you know *exactly* what the offense is. Or the offenses, multiple. The years of abuse, neglect, cruelty. The exact moment of the betrayal. Your body shakes remembering it. You literally see red when you think of it. You have been in a bad mood for years.

These reactions are ruining your life. Maybe you sense that. Maybe you have decided you simply have to live with the pain.

If you are like me, the messages you have heard over the years are about how important it is to forgive. How holy, how Christian. You may have enormous guilt about *not* forgiving. Or you tell yourself you have to love everyone, so there is no one you need to forgive. It took me *a long time* to understand Jesus's commandment to love our enemies, because in my mind I did not have any enemies. I loved everyone! You can see how that attitude kept me from an honest human experience.

You have probably heard the advice that you forgive a person, not for them, but for yourself. Unforgiveness is like wanting to kill a person, but *you* drink the poison. This may be true. We know resentment is bad for our bodies and souls.

You have likely also heard something about forgiving and forgetting. I hate that advice. In many ways we cannot forget the bad thing that happened to us; we need to remember the perpetrator's actions so they cannot hurt us again. "Let's just move on," is rarely a good idea when people are hurting. I find the person who says, "Can't we get past this?" is usually one of the perpetrators and does not want to sit in the guilt any longer.

Has your perpetrator asked for forgiveness? This is an important step as you decide whether you can or want to forgive someone. Have they seen the error of their ways? Are they truly repentant? That matters.

Are they blind to their responsibility? That makes forgiveness so much more difficult. This may be information you need to stay away from that person. They may be dangerous. Or emotionally unavailable. Or simply deficient. This is very painful and can often make a relationship irreparable. Relationship is a two-way street. Yes, Jesus wants us to be in relationships with people, but not to the detriment of ourselves. You may feel this great guilty command to forgive someone who has been horrible to you. But are they asking for it? Or are they simply saying, "Can't we move on?" That is very different from someone who says, "I see we cannot move on until we face this problem."

We keep saying as a society, "We need to have the hard conversation about racism (or homophobia or sexism)." And we all nod and say OK, and then never have the conversation. Talking about forgiveness and reconciliation is not the same as actually forgiving and finding a path to reconciliation. So, saying, "Let's forgive and forget," without doing the work for it is impossible.

Another hinderance is if the person who harmed you is incapacitated. They may be the person you now have to care for. Oof, does this complicate the relationship you have, especially as their care gets more difficult. Now what will you do? Each story is different, each scenario has its own layers. This would be an excellent problem to bring to a professional counselor or therapist. You might long to fight with this person and they cannot speak. Or they have died, with your issues unresolved. This is one of life's cruelest situations. But again, if forgiveness is supposed to be *for you*, there is a path forward. First, name all the things this person did to hurt you. You are going to have to feel all the feelings. Sorry, it is just true. Maybe you can find a way to forgive after that. Maybe you cannot. Maybe you have acceptance. Maybe you do not. In any case, *you matter.* Your feelings are valid, your experience is your experience. Do not let other people take that away from you. Then you get to make some decisions. Will you work to move through the feelings? Are you wanting to just stay in this misery or resentment or anger? It is your timeline—your decision. Are other loved ones seeing these feelings as disruptive? Are you interested in healing for them and yourself? Yes, there are a thousand questions. That is because *you matter.*

Now turn these questions to yourself. Are *you* the one you cannot forgive? Are *you* the one who has hurt yourself or another? Have you made poor choices that have negatively impacted your life? Are you in the caregiving situation you are in now because of things *you* did? Because of responsibilities to which *you* agreed? This has been a very hard part of my story; I blame myself for my difficult life. My wife and I decided to adopt. We had some sense of how hard it would be. And we still did it. I often fret that this miserable life was entirely my fault.

Professionals, family members, my spouse: they have all tried to convince me otherwise. It is not my fault. It is no one's fault. We did not have all the information. People hoped for different outcomes. Life is unfair. It is not my fault.

But this has been the hardest step in my spiritual care: forgiving myself for choices I have made. I have repented for arrogance. I have repented for ignorance. I have repented for hubris. I have repented for . . . what? Tenacity? Commitment? Decency? Foolishness? Blind-spots? Loving too much? Not loving enough?

As with all spiritual needs, it is time to turn to God. Who do we think God is? This is a critical question in our view of God. Is God judgmental or forgiving? Does God bear a grudge, holding us to an impossible standard? Does God shake God's head, muttering about how awful we humans are? Or, does God long for healing and whole-ness? Christians would say God longed for reconciliation and sent Jesus to earth to bring that about. Jesus joined us in our humanity, experiencing all the joy and heartache of human relationship. Human loss, human connection. Jesus preached forgiveness, for each other and from God. Jesus wanted us to live faithfully, and to be as holy as possible. This may sound like Jesus wanted us to live perfectly. Jesus knew that was not possible. Jesus knew the only way we could love perfectly and forgive perfectly was to depend upon God. To take in God's forgiveness, and then to forgive ourselves. Forgive others. This is hard work. This is lifelong work. But can you let in that God wants to forgive? God wants to fill you with God's love and God's spirit, the only things that can make us righteous. God's love is the only thing that lasts eternally, even as we stumble and fail and hurt each other. Part of our spiritual care is to reflect upon this love and forgiveness.

I have often believed Satan's biggest deception is convincing us we are not good enough for God's love. Satan puts a wedge of self-doubt into each of us. Satan convinces us God is furious, will not be soothed. Satan tells us God hates us. This is the biggest lie of all. God does not hate us; God loves us. God loves the world so much God sent Jesus to join with us, to live with us and die with us and show us, over and over again, how much God loves us. God loves us enough to die with us. And then God shows how much God loves us by conquering death, by coming back to life after the crucifixion. God loves us enough to bring eternal life. Why would God want eternal damnation for us? God wants eternal life. This God forgives us. This God forgives our enemies. This is why we say, "to forgive is divine." It is sacred, eternal work.

Some of the work involves simply telling the truth to yourself, or to others, or to God. Probably the work involves telling the truth to all three. I was in a seminarians' support group where we told our personal stories to the group at the beginning of the semester. At the end of the semester, we were invited to tell the stories again. Some of us told them in almost the same manner, with the same details. The places that had been tragic before were still tragic. The places where we became angry still made us angry. But some of us now told our stories in completely new ways. The details were clarified or ignored, depending on what mattered to the teller now. Stories that had been filled with pain and betrayal were now told with compassion and balance. Key points in the first telling were now insignificant, or at least reframed. Other things that had barely been noticed in the first telling were now featured. Healing had happened. For most of us, we had not been aware of this healing. It had happened while we were doing other things. But clearly slights had been forgiven, burdens had been lifted. Sometimes we simply had insights into what the other people in the story must have been going through. Sometimes we had clarity on what *we* had been going through.

Certainly 12-step programs work on this clarity. Clarity often comes through the painful work of taking responsibility for our actions. Clarity comes when we can see which parts were our doing, which parts were the doing of others, and which parts were out of everyone's control. These are difficult things to understand. As mentioned in chapter 3 on guilt, the myth of mastery is a killer. We are fooled into thinking we are in control of our lives. We also think *other* people can be in control of our lives.

We do need to find a balance, though, between giving up control and eschewing all responsibility. As the serenity prayer reminds us, we need to accept the things we cannot change, have courage to change the things we can, and the wisdom to know the difference. We *are* responsible for our behavior. Others are also responsible for their own behavior.

Getting people to take responsibility can be very difficult, if not impossible. Hopefully, if the people wish to be in relationship with us, they will try to take responsibility for their actions. Perhaps at the very least, they will accept the fact that their actions *affect* us. But we know this is not always the case.

The work is figuring out who is responsible for what. Who needs to be forgiven? Who needs to ask for forgiveness? Sometimes it will be you. Sometimes it will be me. Can you come with gentleness, maybe with Jesus at your side, and look at your situation? There are opportunities here, for you to be healed. Remember you are not alone. God is with you, God loves you. And this takes time. Now take a deep breath, get a drink of water, and find something pretty to look at for a few minutes. Repeat as necessary.

CHAPTER FIFTEEN

Complete Surrender

Step one: We admitted we were powerless over our addiction, and that our lives had become unmanageable.

—Step One in the 12-Step Program

This is the chapter where we admit we are powerless. Not over an addiction, but over this life that was handed to us. Do you feel the fight rising within you? Do you feel the need to explain to me that I do not understand the pressure you are under, or the responsibilities you have? Yeah, that's the thing we have to admit we are powerless over. This is going to take a minute, friend. Keep reading.

I thought the moment of letting go would be very violent. I thought my will would have to be wrested from my hands; that I would scream and yell and protest vehemently. I was holding in a lot, and I knew I would not let it go easily.

I suppose each of us comes to this moment differently. Some are strong, or "strong-willed" and can hold burdens a very long time. Think of Luisa in *Encanto*. Her strength was her identity, her gift. And it was killing her.

Some have been told, since they were very young, or by someone who matters a great deal in adulthood, that they have no choice but to carry the weight of the world. "It is what we do," they have been told. Or, "If you love me, you will do this." Or, "Only bad people avoid their responsibilities." I recently had a person say to me, "You *never* walk away from family and friends." She thought it was a positive statement, something to be proud of. But I wondered how many times she had been told that in her life, how often that phrase was used in negative ways, how much shame or threat was attached to it. "No matter what happens, *do not* walk away."

But the truth is, sometimes we need to walk away from family and friends. Maybe only for a half hour. To go to your own doctor's appointment. To drink a cup of tea. To look at the sunset. This vast world: its beauty, its comforts, were meant for you too. Everyone deserves to take in the good of the world. Everyone. The wicked, the exhausted, the hopeless, the over-extended, the selfish. God intended the sun to shine on them as well. God wants us all to look up occasionally, feel the warmth on our face, breathe in some fresh air, listen to the wind in the trees. The cacophony of our lives, the noise, the demands, the worry: it is real. The symphony of our day—whether it feels like a punk rock concert, blaring horns, an annoyingly out-of-tune guitar solo, or maybe the drip, drip, drip of a leaky faucet, whatever it is that over-stimulates our brains—*must* include rest notes. Music is not music unless it has both sound and quiet. Life is not life without sound and quiet. Life needs stimulation and rest. We do not function without both. At some point our bodies break down, requiring rest. How often do we hear of a caregiver or other over-functioning person who suddenly breaks a leg, or comes down with a cold, or gets into a car accident, and someone wryly says, "I guess God was just trying to get you to slow down." I do not think God operates in quite that manner, but I do know this is one of the more frequently used bedside expressions. It is one of our human ways to acknowledge we would not lay down our responsibilities unless an outside force intervenes.

But having an outside intervention is a temporary situation. Surrender needs to come from within. Consider the type A personality CEO working from a hospital bed, or a stalwart caregiver finding a way to clean the house on crutches. Both would congratulate themselves on their tenacity. The external force that knocked them down was not able to keep them down. It is only when we make a personal conviction that a permanent change can happen. An internal force must make us lay down our responsibility.

The problem is we believe we *are in control*. I should state this a different way: We have fooled ourselves into thinking we are in control. We convince ourselves we get to dictate our own circumstances.

Many readers know something about 12-step programs like Alcoholics Anonymous or Alateen. These programs help people live their lives in more healthy ways. Step one is: "We have come to understand we are powerless . . ." We have come to realize we must surrender. We must give up the idea that we are in control of . . . anything but ourselves. And for you control freaks out there, you still get to be in control of something. It's just ourselves, and nothing, nothing, nothing else.

This is a long struggle, to figure out what we can control and what we cannot. "God grant me the serenity to accept the things I cannot change . . ." This is a confusing, difficult understanding to come to, and honestly, I'm going to blame our parents for some of this. Our parents, the really gifted loving ones, and the horribly neglectful cruel ones, believed they had power over us long past the early years when we were completely dependent upon them. Or they abdicated their responsibility to us while we were still completely dependent, which confused our boundaries and understanding of the world in other complicated ways. Very few of our parents got the balance of responsibility and release right. Who could blame them? Well, me. Sorry, Mom and Dad.

We leave home and society gets its hook into us. In an effort to teach us how to behave, we are told we can control our consequences. The message is projected frequently: "If you are good, good things will happen to you. If you are bad, bad things will happen to you." I cannot decide if it is a blessing or a curse to learn about life's randomness at an early age. Is it better for a child to know bad things happen to good people (and good things happen to bad people) or is it best if they are spared that cruel lesson for a while? In any case, we all must come to terms with this fact: no matter how we live or what we do, we cannot control all outcomes. There are many, many things over which we have no power. Is this making you angry, or is the truth setting you free?

At the top of the list of things we cannot control is other people. We might care for the infirm, but we cannot make them take care of themselves, we cannot make them be grateful, we cannot make them healthy. Ask the frustrated grandfather how hard it is to *make* a three-year-old take a nap. Ask the broken-hearted Romeo how hard it is to *make* his paramour fall in love with him. Of course, people have forced others to do things, in war, slavery, and manipulation, but no good relationships ever come from that.

But my darling controlling types, we *can* control our own actions. We can make good choices about how we behave. Step one might be to control our feelings. Oops, just kidding. We cannot control our feelings. Those suckers just come up whenever they want. It's messy and potentially embarrassing and frequently annoying, but we cannot control our emotions. We *can* learn to control how we react to those emotions. We can be really angry, but we can learn not to destroy property or hurt people. We can be truly hurt, but we can learn not to lash out to "even the score." We can be extremely nervous or excited, and learn not to talk everyone's ear off, or eat everything in the house, or self-medicate with alcohol or drugs. This emotional work takes a lot of time, a lot of patience, a lot of grace. Ugh, that's another book entirely.

I will tell you a little about my own moment of total surrender. It was a long time coming. I did not wake up one morning and say, "OK, I'm done." First there was an enormous amount of grieving that needed to take place. I had to grieve all the expectations I had for my life. I expected my relationships to go a certain way. I even expected my relationships to be difficult, but I expected my own gifts to fill in the gaps. I expected to meet adversity with wisdom and grace and humor. I am so funny! Laughter can cure many ills. But there are a hell of a lot of ills that laughter cannot cure. That was a painful lesson to learn.

My understanding of my own superhuman abilities had to be torn down. I am not significantly better at caregiving or patience or creative thinking than other people. I was pretty sure I was. Get called "gifted" or "talented" or "special" enough times as a child and you spend a lifetime trying to achieve an accurate self-assessment.

I have quite a bit of self-awareness, but that is both a blessing and a curse. I was aware of the feelings I was having, which *may* have helped me come to terms with them more quickly, but it also made life messier and more complicated as I had to greet each feeling individually and face it. Yuck. And ouch, damn it, ouch. It is a difficult balance, having enough ego strength to do the hard work of tearing down your ego.

Along with all the grieving, I had a lot of resentment. I spent several months complaining about my miserable life. How did this happen to *me?* I am a good person, only wanting to do the right thing, and this is the life I end up with? Yes, this is also part of grieving, but it took a lot of mental space, this anger about the injustice of it all. I think this is another necessary step. I thought I would still be in this step when the surrender came, that the universe or God or some other force would be wrenching my personality and my will out of my cold, dead hands. I expected a bloody fight at the end, after which I would angrily throw down some sort of gauntlet and say, "Fine! You win!!!" and be furious. I would begrudgingly march off to some sort of psychological prisoner of war camp, shooting dirty looks at my captors for the rest of my days. I would always be searching for an escape route. I would always be plotting a new way to get back in control. Yes, it would be surrender, but boy, would it be ugly.

If you suspect surrender looks like that, you are not quite done with the process. This should be good news to you: surrender will not feel like the other side of the bitter coin you are currently fingering. It will feel better. Well, maybe not better. Maybe just different.

There is a peace in this place of surrender I did not expect. I do not feel empty, per se. But I feel quieter. I am not depleted. I am certainly not defeated. Maybe I would say a weight has been lifted, but that does not feel like an accurate description either. Maybe the weight has moved off my shoulders and now occupies the seat next to me in a fairly small space.

"Space" seems to be an important part of surrender. My shape has changed, not physically, but metaphorically. Think of the descriptions I have written throughout the book: bent-over woman, invisible caregiver. Burdened. Exhausted. When we give up some of this weight, our shape changes. We occupy space, spiritual space, differently.

After a particularly bad night in my house, I sat on my bed. I was angry, exhausted, frustrated, despairing. I had been trying to release my life to my higher power, but I was still holding on to all the feelings, all the responsibility.

My prayer was brief. "God, where *are* you?"

The air in the room immediately became very heavy, like a weight pushing down around me. It was not unpleasant, but it was oppressive. Maybe not oppressive. All-encompassing. Nowhere to go where the pressure was not around me, embracing me. Yes. Embracing me. An invisible force, thick, heavy, entirely surrounding me. It lifted after a moment. I believe I got my answer to the question, "God where are you?" God was everywhere. There is nowhere to go where God is not. But sometimes God is invisible.

It is a miserable truth. It is also the mystery of our faith. God does what God wants. We can fight against that. We humans have been arguing with God about God's plan since the garden of Eden.

There is a wonderful joke: What's the difference between you and God? God never thinks God is you.

And that is the truth of surrender. We have to give up the idea that we are God. We do not take up the space God takes up. Many of us would say, "Of course I know I am not God," and then we realize we expected miracles to happen because we were noble. If we are honest, we thought if we quit our job and stayed up all night, our sick father would not die. We thought if we threw enough money at her, our daughter would no longer be an addict. We thought if we lost all that weight, our marriage would be saved. I once realized I thought if I did what God wanted a dead friend would come back to life. Of course, I had not *really* said those words out loud to myself, but later it became clear I was expecting that kind of miracle. Have you had unrealistic expectations about what your actions can accomplish? Ready to throw this book across the room again?

There is wisdom and peace in finding our limitations. There is communion and strength in discovering where we end, and another begins. There is truth and beauty in finding the distinctions between our personal shape and God's shape.

We have been taught the sin of Adam and Eve was eating the fruit of the tree of the knowledge of good and evil. We believe their sin was simply disobeying God's commandment. The story tells us if they ate that fruit, they would become like God. They would understand the differences in the world between good and evil. This sin was more than just disobedience. Their sin was wanting to be like God. We have been committing that sin ever since.

What's the difference between you and God? God never thinks God is you.

CHAPTER SIXTEEN

The Search for God

Then the word of the Lord came to Elijah, saying, "What are you doing here, Elijah?" He answered, "I have been very zealous for the Lord, the God of hosts, for the Israelites have forsaken your covenant, thrown down your altars, and killed your prophets with the sword. I alone am left, and they are seeking my life, to take it away."

And God said, "Go out and stand on the mountain before the Lord, for the Lord is about to pass by." Now there was a great wind, so strong that it was splitting mountains and breaking rocks in pieces before the Lord, but the Lord was not in the wind, and after the wind an earthquake, but the Lord was not in the earthquake, and after the earthquake a fire, but the Lord was not in the fire, and after the fire a sound of sheer silence. When Elijah heard it, he wrapped his face in his mantle and went out and stood at the entrance of the cave. Then there came a voice to him that said, "What are you doing here, Elijah?" He answered, "I have been very zealous for the Lord, the God of hosts, for the Israelites have forsaken your covenant, thrown down your altars, and killed your prophets with the sword. I alone am left, and they are seeking my life, to take it away."

—1 Kings 19:8–14

That's really the kicker, isn't it? Where the hell is God in all this madness? Our life has emotional earthquakes, physical windstorms, spiritual firestorms. Where is God in a violent home? Where is God in the deterioration of an aging mother's brain? Where is God in the death of a child? Where is God when the clock ticks loudly through the night and we cannot sleep because of the dread of tomorrow or the regret of yesterday? Where is God?

The psalmist promises us that if we travel to the east or west, God is there. Highest mountain, deepest valley, God is there. For some of us this sounds more like a threat than a promise:

You can't run away from me! Hee hee! I see you, no matter what!

This can cause great dread, resentment, and a feeling of oppression. God! Get off my back!

It can also bring relief. No matter how far we wander, God is there. No matter how deep the hole is where we live, God is there. If you picture the path you are on right now—seriously, close your eyes and imagine the path you are on—what does it look like?

I think this is a helpful exercise. At one point in my life the path I pictured was a barren desert. No life in sight. There *was* a path, which was encouraging, but man, did it stretch forever with no destination revealed, no towns along the way. I would be alone for a very long time with no water, no rest, no company.

Pretty bleak path. And it is the only image I had for months.

You may see a narrow trail up a high hill. You may picture being stuck in horrible traffic. Sometimes I just picture myself jogging. Long distance. Not too fast, but plodding along, steady rhythm. In that vision, it's less about the destination and more about my ability to keep going. Sometimes I have this image when things are difficult, sometimes I have this image when things are unclear. I'm just jogging along.

But picture that path. Maybe it is beautiful, maybe it is vast, maybe it is a narrow space. A dripping black cave wall. A sunny hillside. The walk up to your front door. A nice walk on the beach. Now realize that no matter what that path looks like, ugly, treacherous, bleak, bountiful, lush, occupied, read these words from Psalm 139:8–12:

> If I ascend to heaven, you are there;
> if I make my bed in Sheol, you are there.
> If I take the wings of the morning
> and settle at the farthest limits of the sea,
> even there your hand shall lead me,
> and your right hand shall hold me fast.
> If I say, "Surely the darkness shall cover me,
> and the light around me become night,"
> even the darkness is not dark to you;
> the night is as bright as the day,
> for darkness is as light to you.

Remember that annoying question some smug Christians ask: "If God feels far away, who moved?" This psalm tells us God is never far away. We may not be able to feel God's presence. That might be because we have become so distracted with our own worries or agendas or anger, we cannot feel God's presence. But to suggest we have moved into a place where God is absent is not helpful. I would also argue it is not possible.

But it is true we cannot always feel God. It is true we often wonder where God can be in all the pain we feel. Martin Luther loved to talk about *Deus absconditus*, the God who has absconded, or is hidden. This is the God to whom I relate.

Hidden God.

Still present. Just not revealing Godself.

Frustrating God.

Jesus would have a lot to say about *Deus absconditus*, as that seems to be the God at the cross. Hidden. Even Jesus had to cry out, "My God, my God, why have you forsaken me?"

Why are you hiding?

Sometimes it comforts me to remember even Jesus wondered where God was. Then I remember this was during Jesus's horrific death, and I do not wish to relate so much to him. But the experience of not knowing where God is is real, is normal, happens literally to the best of us.

Why does God hide? In the case of Jesus's death, some would suggest God was hiding so Satan would mistakenly think he had won. And then when Jesus rose from the dead, the victory was all that much sweeter because Satan was humiliated. Perhaps God hides to be mysterious, and to demand we trust in God's unknowable ways. You might expect God would show up like a superhero during our dark hours. Later we realized God is revealed in the suffering, not in the saving. God is a small, still voice, not a hurricane.

If you are in the middle of crisis while reading this, you may not find comfort in these words. You may be convinced God has left the building, has been distracted by some war somewhere, had a bunch of baby seals to save. You suspected you were not good enough for God's attention, and this moment in time *proves it.*

What does it feel like if you imagine God is with you, but God is hiding? It might outrage you. You might mention that to God. It might amuse you, as if God is a playful child. It might confound you. Again, tell that to God. What if you can imagine God is hiding but God will be revealed at some point? In the meantime, God is watching, knowing, loving.

Let's go back to Psalm 139: "Even the darkness is not dark to you; the night is as bright as the day."

So even when we feel like we are in utter darkness, it is bright as day to God. Why is that helpful?

Yes, it would be *fantastic* if God would simply turn on the light and let us get our bearings. I cannot explain why God does not do that. I can tell you God usually does *not* do that. God may send someone to stand in the dark with us. God may send someone to pull you out of the dark room. God may light a candle. But rarely does God simply turn the lights on and everything is perfect.

But there is a bit of method to God's madness. Early on in our covenant relationship with God, back in the Moses/Mount Sinai time, God explained a little something about God's self. God and Moses spent days together, but Moses did not get to look at God directly. Here is an excerpt from your favorite book of the Bible, Deuteronomy:

> So watch your conduct closely, because you didn't see any form on the day the Lord spoke to you at Horeb out of the very fire itself.
> Don't ruin everything and make an idol for yourself:
> A form of any image, any likeness—male or female—
> or any likeness whatsoever,
> whether of a land animal,
> a bird that flies in the sky,
> an insect that crawls on the earth,
> or a fish that lives in the sea.
> Don't . . . be led astray,
> worshipping and serving them. (Deut 4:16–19)

So, God says, "Remember, Moses, when you were up on the mountain and getting the law? I would not let you see me. Because if you did see me, you would come running back down the hill and try to make an idol that looked like me, and soon you would be worshipping that image of me, rather than just worshipping *me*."

God knows we would not do well with knowing what God looked like. We would start trying to draw pictures, make statues, dress up in costumes, all these things that would remind us of God's image. God has been clear about no graven images and the like.

So, no images of God, no knowing what God looks like. Because God knew we would mess that up. The Jewish faith, which is adamant about no graven images, likes to say that "God is unknowable." I find comfort in that. I should stop trying to understand God. How about I just love God, maybe even "fear" God as the old language goes. Fearing God might just be honoring and obeying but never truly understanding.

Which, perhaps, gets to the heart of this chapter. God is revealed in surprising, maddening ways. If God had one way of operating, we would come to expect it. We would "know" it. And the knowing is a form of idolatry, I suspect. If we can count on God's revelation to be one specific way all the time, we might worship that, instead of the Unknowable One Who Surprises Us.

In the meantime, if you are not sure where God is, sit still for a while. Maybe God will find you. Maybe God has been right here all along. Too tired to pray? Ask someone else to do it. Too angry to pray? Tell God that. And maybe nothing else. Too sad to pray? Been there. Cry a lot and tell God that is all you got. God can take it or leave it. I truly believe God will take it. Oh, this is a lonely, beautiful, painful, bittersweet journey we are on. You are not alone. You have God. You have your big beautiful, exhausted heart. And you have this reservoir of love and hope and tenderness and care. You may know it is empty right now. But God can fill you up. And when you cannot believe it, there are thousands of others, millions, if you count the communion of saints who have gone before us, who will believe on your behalf until you are able to experience God's closeness again.

God is unknowable, but trustworthy. Consistent and dynamic. Just like us. Just like life. You know more about God than you realize. And God knows, and loves, everything about you.

Acknowledgments

If you've understood anything from this book, you understand it takes a village to be a human. It also takes a village to be a human who cares for humans. First and foremost, I thank my wife, Janis Reid, for being my co-conspirator, twin mama bear, and fierce champion. I thank the amazing parents and professionals I have met as we learned to care for our son, especially Sean Sparks and Jill Mattinson-Cruz. Gratitude to the FASD Support Network of Southern California and all professional organizations working for justice and care of the most vulnerable. My spiritual directors, Philippa Curry and Rev. Dr. Duane Bidwell, kept my head above water—get yourself a spiritual director. My coaches, Rozella Haydée White, Dr. Dee Littleton, and Dawn Trautman, give me so much hope and focus—get yourself a coach. I've got a chorus of therapists and pastors: you know who you are, and you know your influence. And then the friends, too many to mention, but the key contributors to my writing of this book: Susan Avallone and Laurie Parres, who knew me long before my career as a pastor, and believed in this book years before it was written; Desta Goehner, Amalia Vagts, Heidi Beth Fisher, Asher O'Callaghan, Tuhina Rasche, and my "Mike B," Brian Landau. To my mom and her friends who thought I was brilliant as a junior high kid on stage, to my dad who understood more than I ever dreamed, and to every person who heard even a titch of my story and simply offered a look of recognition: thank you. Steven Hall, copy editor to the stars, you have the patience of a saint. To Deacon Dr. Laura Gifford, my editor at Fortress Press, thanks for being the smartest person in the room. Let's do this again real soon.

And to my son, who made me a mother, who insisted we have a zombie apocalypse plan, who broke my heart open and showed me my strengths and weaknesses: your superpower is hope.